Hamlyn all-colour paperbacks

Frederick Wilkinson

Guns

illustrated by Michael Shoebridge

D0993385

Hamlyn · London
Sun Books · Melbourne

FOREWORD

Perhaps the romantic streak in many of us gives a special appeal to an antique firearm, conjuring up an association with highwaymen, pirates, cowboys and the Redcoats. However, a slightly closer study of any of these weapons will soon reveal a history which began over a thousand years ago in China where an unknown inventor mixed three chemicals together. He could not have foreseen the impact that this mixture was to have on the world, for this compound was gunpowder.

The first crude firearms made their appearance in Europe early in the fourteenth century. At first they were unreliable and ineffective, but slowly their design and power increased and by the sixteenth century they were beginning to dominate the battlefields. From then on, their story became more and more involved with inventors seeking ways to improve the performance of firearms. Some of the characters were remarkable people and some of the new ideas strange; one man wanted to fire round bullets at Christians and square ones at Turks.

Gradually the firearm changed from a hand-made craftsman's job to the mass-produced item of the nineteenth century. But still the search to improve its performance went on. Accuracy was improved by rifling the barrel; performance was increased by the use of metal cartridges, and by the end of the nineteenth century, magazine rifles were commonplace. The fascinating story of the emergence of the modern firearm is traced in detail in this book, and the full-colour illustrations show clearly the beauty and mechanical ingenuity of a wide range of weapons.

F.W.

Published by The Hamlyn Publishing Group Limited
London · New York · Sydney · Toronto
Hamlyn House, Feltham, Middlesex, England
In association with Sun Books Pty Ltd Melbourne

Copyright © The Hamlyn Publishing Group Limited 1970

ISBN 0 690 00290 X
Phototypeset by Jolly & Barber Limited, Rugby, Warwickshire
Colour separations by Schwitter Limited, Zurich
Printed in England by Sir Joseph Causton & Sons Limited

CONTENTS

4 Ancient artillery
8 Gunpowder
10 Early cannon
16 Early handguns
21 The matchlock
29 The wheel-lock
45 The snaphaunce
48 The flintlock
89 The percussion gun
108 The breech-loader
150 Gun manufacture
153 Decoration
154 Modern weapons
156 Books to read
157 Index

The trebuchet *(left)* could hurl stones weighing two or three hundredweight. The machine *(right)* is a spring engine.

ANCIENT ARTILLERY

Man's first missile was nothing more than a hand-hurled stone. But soon he progressed to spears and to these he gave added impetus by means of a spear thrower. These devices, no more than a stick with a notched end, extended the length of his throwing arm and so supplied greater power.

Stones and spears cast by hand were of little use in siege warfare and thus man sought mechanized means to increase the range and size of missile. One of the most powerful siege weapons was the trebuchet which could cast large boulders over a considerable distance. These weapons consisted of a long arm weighted at one end by a heavy box of earth or rock and pivoted at the centre. Wound down by capstan, the unweighted end was loaded with a stone and when the arm was released the counterbalance depressed the arm violently to send the load whistling through the air.

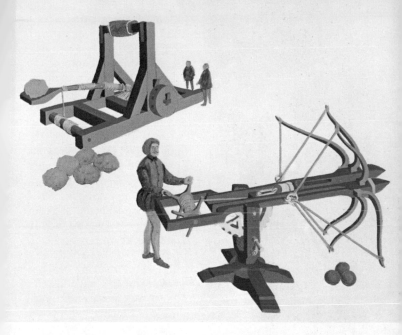

Both the catapult *(left)* and the ballista *(right)* were medieval survivors of the siegecraft of the Romans

Trebuchets did sterling service until ousted by gunpowder, battering walls and bombarding towns with rocks or occasionally filth and carrion to spread disease. Catapults of many designs were also used and these, like the trebuchets, were usually constructed on the site from materials to hand. Catapults obtained their force from twisted ropes rather than counterbalancing weights. They had an arm which was embedded in a skein of plaited ropes. When the arm was pulled down to the horizontal position the rope developed great torque. On release the arm swung through a right angle to hurl its projectile into the air.

The same principle was used in the Roman ballista in which twisted ropes were used to supply motive power to twin arms which, together, formed a crossbow-like device. Ballistas were used to fire javelins. The spring engine was another missile weapon using the flexibility of wood as a source of power.

Missile weapons

Slings, used by foot soldiers from earliest times, were simply miniature versions of the catapult; some were patches on thongs but others, more powerful, were fitted at the end of a long staff.

Far more lethal was the long-bow which, in the hands of an expert archer, could drive an arrow through armour and mail. The English long-bow was about six feet long, over an inch in diameter at the centre and required a pull of eighty to a hundred pounds to bend it. These great bows could send an arrow, about one yard long and fletched with goose feathers, accurately over considerable distances. Each archer normally carried about two dozen arrows in a quiver or tucked under his belt and in battle could maintain a steady stream of shafts. Arrow heads were small and designed to deliver the maximum impact on the smallest area to give greatest penetration.

A well-trained man could achieve considerable accuracy with medieval missile weapons, even with such simple ones as the sling *(bottom, left)*. The long-bow *(top, left)* could have a range of 400 yards but required much more skill in its use than the crossbow *(opposite)*.

However, constant practice was essential to ensure accurate aiming from the archer.

More powerful than the long-bow and simpler to use was the crossbow. Despite its greater penetrative power and greater simplicity of use it did suffer from one great drawback – a slow rate of fire. During the time it took a crossbowman to fire one bolt, an archer could loose six to twelve arrows.

Early crossbows had wooden bows which could be bent by normal manual strength but to increase range and power, composite and, later on, steel bows were used. So great was their strength that mechanical devices like the windlass, cranequin and goatsfoot levers had to be used. Arrows were short with broad heads and flighted with feathers or leather and were carried in a rectangular quiver. When the bow was spanned the cord engaged with a simple retaining device, the nut, which was released by a long bar which served as a trigger. The bolt was placed in a shallow groove and the bow was aimed in much the same way as the later firearms. Of course, these operations all took some time to carry out.

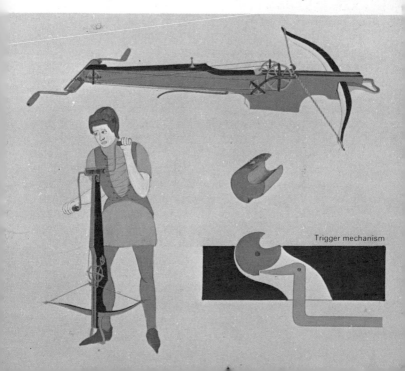

Trigger mechanism

(Above) two arrow-firing hand-guns, one Chinese, c. 1621, and one Arabic. (Right) Friar Bacon. (Opposite page) the legendary Black Berthold was depicted in many prints and drawings.

GUNPOWDER

Legends, fables and traditions have long been associated with the discovery of gunpowder and many races have been credited with its original discovery. Modern research has demolished most of these highly colourful explanations and the general belief is that gunpowder was first known in China.

All the evidence suggests that a weak explosive compound was in use in Cathay in the early part of the eleventh century. Its purpose was primarily to provide noise, smoke and flash and it also powered crude rockets. During the second quarter of the twelfth century it is clear that a crude form of handgun, fashioned from reinforced bamboo, was being used by the Chinese. Such a gun is shown at the top of this page.

Knowledge of this wondrous mixture of saltpetre, sulphur and charcoal was acquired by the Arabs who passed it on to Europe, but at what date is not at all certain. The evidence is confusing and unclear. One name firmly associated with the discovery of gunpowder is that of Roger Bacon, a cleric with a scientific curiosity in natural phenomena. He wrote several books around the middle of the thirteenth century and in a printed edition of his work dated 1618 there appears a sentence or two that have been interpreted as containing an anagram for the formula of gunpowder. This might well be acceptable as proof but for the fact that this particular section does not occur in the earliest known copy of Bacon's book and another manuscript of the fifteenth century contains a different version of the 'gunpowder' anagram. However other evidence

does seem to suggest that Bacon was at least familiar with the effects of gunpowder even if he did not discover it.

Another claim of even greater doubtfulness is that of the friar of Frieberg – Berthold. The story runs that one day as Berthold was experimenting in his laboratory he compounded the elements of gunpowder. An accidental spark ignited it and the resulting explosion sent the lid or pestle flying from his hand and so inspired him to advance the idea of firearms hurling projectiles. The town later erected a statue in honour of the monk who, in fact, may never have existed.

Walter de Milemete's manuscript showed a cannon, probably of brass, at the moment of firing. *(Below)* a cannon and recoil plate, c.1350.

EARLY CANNON

If the date of the first knowledge of gunpowder in Europe is doubtful the date of its first practical application is equally uncertain. So far, the earliest traced reference occurs in the records of the City Republic of Florence, which in 1326 state that two men were to be paid to produce metal bullets, arrows and cannon for the city's defence.

The first pictorial evidence is supplied by a manuscript written in 1326 by Walter de Milemete for Edward III in which there is a clear and positive representation of a vase-like cannon. There is, unfortunately, no reference to the drawing in the text but there can be no doubt that it is a cannon. An armoured knight is shown igniting the charge of powder contained in a, presumably, metal barrel from which protrudes the point of an arrow.

Many of these early firearms were used to discharge arrows, and such missiles were still listed among the stores of the

Tower of London as late as the seventeenth century. Confirmation of this shape of early gun has been supplied by excavated specimens, although a more conventional, cylindrical barrel was soon produced and became general.

From the middle of the fourteenth century onwards references to firearms increase in the records of the period but their use was largely restricted to siege work. Castles were immensely strong and capable of resisting, for long periods, the effect of siege machines. A cannon once made could be used continuously, with less effort than the older projectile arms, to batter enormous walls and towers.

Ammunition was provided locally from suitable stone which could be sculptured into great balls and these were undoubtedly used far more frequently than iron, which was expensive to supply and difficult to mould. The powder presented certain problems and hazards. If the compound was made as a simple mixture it was found that any protracted

A detail from a 16th-century painting showing two guns with wooden carriages and stone cannon-balls

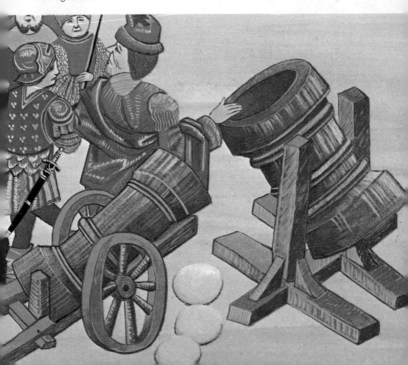

bumping and jolting tended to separate each of the components into layers. Thus the explosive quality could well depend on how far the powder had been transported. There was also the ever-present danger of an accidental explosion for there were frequent eruptions of sparks and glowing embers. Gunners were often viewed with as much displeasure by their allies as by their enemies.

Early cannon were not cast in a mould but were constructed in a variety of ways. Probably the commonest involved the use of bars and hoops; the bars were placed side by side around a former and then hoops, heated to a high temperature, were slipped over the bars and pushed up side by side. As the hoops cooled they contracted and so forced the whole mass into a solid barrel strong enough to resist most explosions.

Soon the gunfounders were sufficiently skilful to cast the barrel in one, although there were potential dangers in this

An English breech-loader of the mid-15th century, three feet long and weighing 125 lbs. A number of loaded chambers could be made ready to maintain a rapid rate of fire. Chambers such as these were held in position by wedges or similar devices.

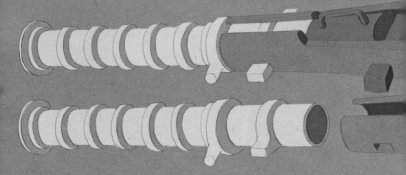

system. If the metal cooled unevenly internal stresses
set up which could well result in the barrel bursting aft.. a
number of shots.

It was not an infrequent occurrence for guns to explode; in
1460 at the siege of Roxburgh James II of Scotland lost his life
in just such an accident.

Most of the earliest cannon were fashioned in two sections –
the barrel and the chamber. Each barrel had a number of
associated chambers which were basically no more than metal
mugs with a small hole drilled through one side. Each chamber
was filled with an appropriate charge of powder and on top of
this was placed a wad and ball. The loaded chamber was then
positioned behind the rear, or breech, end of the barrel and
held firmly in place usually by driving home wedges of wood
between the base of the chamber and a stout retaining block
firmly secured to a base block. A piece of glowing coal, moss,

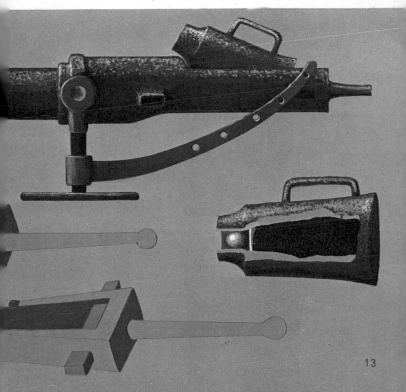

Mons Meg, in Edinburgh, certainly of Flemish origin, weighs five tons

or tow was then placed over the touch hole piercing the side of the chamber, the charge was ignited and the cannon fired. The wedges were removed, a new charged chamber placed in position and the cannon was ready to fire another round.

As the gunfounder gained in skill he was able to produce larger barrels capable of hurling enormous balls over quite considerable distances. Some of these early cannon have survived and have acquired a variety of names and legends.

One of the most famous is the large cannon still at Edinburgh Castle and known as Mons Meg. According to early records this great piece of ordnance took a charge of more than one hundred pounds of powder which was rammed firmly home into the chamber. On top of the powder went a ball nearly twenty inches in diameter. With the barrel tilted up at an angle of 45° Meg would hurl a stone ball 2867 yards, although a heavier iron ball would only go 1408 yards.

Meg saw service during some of the Scottish wars but met a somewhat ignominious end when the side split during the firing of a salute in honour of the birthday of James II when he was Duke of York. After lying neglected for many years, the cannon was sent to the Tower of London but was returned to the castle in 1829 and finally mounted on a carriage which is a facsimile of one shown on a stone panel carved during the late sixteenth century or early seventeenth century.

Meg was indeed made at Mons in 1449 and sent, as a gift to Scotland, by the Duke of Burgundy. Jehan Combier, a master craftsman, supervised the construction of this fifteen feet long piece with a bore of eighteen inches.

Another monster gun is the one known as the Dardanelles gun and which, at present, stands in the grounds of Her Majesty's Tower of London. It is again a giant, measuring seventeen feet long with a bore of 25 inches, but what makes this weapon rather unusual is that it is fashioned in two pieces which are cut with a giant thread so that the two sections may be screwed together. It was thought, at one time, that the purpose of this arrangement was to facilitate loading, but the effort required to rotate the considerable weight would suggest that it was so designed for ease of transport.

The Dardanelles gun was cast in 1464, though cannon of the same type saw service at Mohammed II's seige of Constantinople in 1453.

The Dardanelles Gun, weighing 18¾ tons, fired a shot of 800 lbs. It was cast in bronze in 1464. The cross-section diagram *(above)* shows the breech and the touch hole.

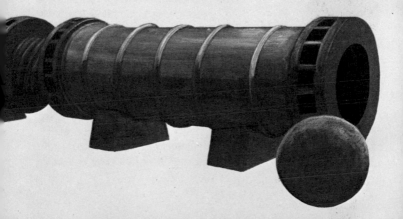

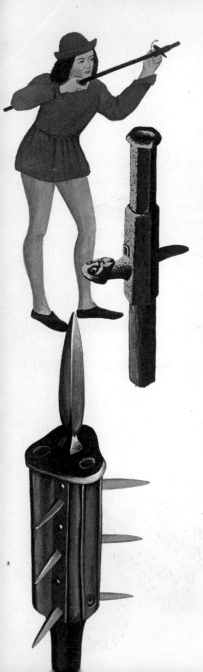

The bronze hand-cannon *(top left)* dates from the late 14th century. It was fired by a touch hole, as in full-sized guns, and had a barrel 7½ inches long. *(Bottom)* a multi-barrelled hand-cannon and mace combination.

EARLY HANDGUNS

It was not long before the 'gonnes' were playing a far more important role on the battlefields of Europe. Soon the makers were experimenting with the concept of a smaller version of the cannon – one that could be carried by one man. It was a simple matter to cast a small version of the barrel but the use of separate chambers presented a far more complex problem. Although it is likely that a few small guns were cast with separate chambers none have survived.

With these handguns, the powder was poured in through the muzzle as was the ball of stone, iron or lead. The technique for firing these hand cannon was exactly the same as for the larger version and some form of glowing tip was placed in the touch hole to ignite the powder.

Obviously it was hardly practical to hold these weapons in the hand and the armourer gave the firer some protection by fitting the small

(Right) examples of early hand-guns. *(From the top)* a crude iron gun, 14th century; a brass gun; a hand mortar. *(Below)* a cannoneer with handcannon mounted on a tiller.

barrel at the end of a wooden or metal stock.

Some handguns were secured to the wooden stock, or tiller, by a series of thongs or metal straps, but more sophisticated models were cast with long sockets which fitted over the end of the wooden bar. Occasionally existing weapons were modified to take the addition of a handgun; some were made with two or more barrels.

Spiked clubs were made with three-inch barrels each with its own touch hole, but whether it was planned as a gun which could be used as a club or a club which could be used as a gun is not at all clear. With any explosion there is a backward jerk – the recoil – and with any firearm this presents a problem. Early gunmakers overcame the problem by fitting the bar with a hook beneath the barrel which was placed over the top of a wall to absorb much of the shock. This type was known in Germany as *Hakenbüchse,* a name anglicized to Arquebus.

Adapted from a Latin manuscript of c.1400, this picture shows a cavalryman with a 'sciopetto' firing lead shot

Early handguns were anything but reliable and, because of their design, almost impossible to aim. Even had they been aimed, the problems of ballistics involved and the gunners' lack of knowledge would still have made the path of the bullet largely a matter of chance.

Despite these obvious limitations the introduction of gunpowder and handguns was to change the entire science of warfare. Prior to this event the knight had feared only the archer for, in general terms, he was the most likely to pierce the protective shell of armour with which the knight encased himself. The crossbow was extremely powerful and could drive a bolt through all but the very thickest of armour; however it had a slow rate of fire and was difficult to make. The long-bow was far less complicated and gave a greater rate of fire, but required years of practice to master its use, as well as a degree of physical strength and endurance not possessed by all.

Handguns had a slow rate of fire but the bullet was capable of penetrating armour. Their greatest virtues were simplicity and cheapness. Numbers could be cast without due hardship, but, best of all, little or no skill was required in their use. Certainly a fair degree of luck was needed to hit a target with one shot but a large number of almost untrained men could create a barrage which must, in the law of averages, have caused a number of casualties. No longer was the armourer able to offer guaranteed protection.

Handguns were fired in a variety of stances. Contemporary illustrations show them being used with the end of the stock pressed firmly against the chest, tucked under the arm, pushed into the ground and supported by a tripod. To guard against accidental loss some were fitted with a ring which was secured by a cord or chain around the knight's neck. Guns ousted the older weapons and by the late sixteenth century long-bows were obsolete although crossbows were still used for hunting.

Cannon, bows and arrows, and handguns all had a part in the siege warfare of the 15th century

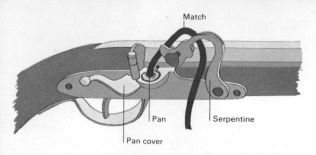

The mechanism of the matchlock

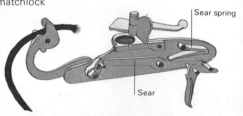

The soldier *(below)* carries a triple-barrelled matchlock, one of the weapons in the arsenals of Emperor Maximilian I, drawn by Nicholaus Glockenthon, c.1505.

(Above) early 17th-century musketeer. *(Below)* a *landsknecht* of the early 16th century rams a charge down his musket barrel.

THE MATCHLOCK

One severe limitation on the soldier equipped with a hand-gun was the means of ignition; if a heated wire or glowing embers were used, it was essential to have a fire within reasonable distance.

Late in the fourteenth century somebody had the idea of using a form of cord which would burn slowly with a glowing end like a large candle wick. It was soon found that this effect was easily obtained if the cord were first soaked in a mixture containing saltpetre and then allowed to dry.

The advent of the match rendered the soldier freer to move about but it was still no easy task in the heat of battle to locate the small touch hole with the tip of the match. A simple mechanical system known as the serpentine was devised which was basically a double curved arm pivoted at the centre and secured to the side of the gun stock. Into the top arm was fitted the glowing end of the match. Pressure on the lower section caused the top arm to move forward and down to place the glowing end on the touch hole.

The musket

With the appearance of the serpentine the handgun was set to develop into a far more sophisticated and useful weapon. Experience soon taught that accuracy and power improved if a long barrel was used, and soon most barrels were as much as four or five feet long.

In place of the early touch hole situated on the top of the barrel, the hole was moved to the side of the barrel and a small platform fitted just level with it. Into a saucer-shaped depression on this side lug, the pan, went a pinch of fine gunpowder, the priming. When the match touched the priming it flared up and so was far more likely to ignite the main charge.

As the barrel was lengthened so the wooden body, the stock, was also lengthened and the portion at the breech end was shaped to allow the weapon to be raised and rested against the shoulder. It was possible for the user to take some form of aim, and barrels were soon fitted with sights. For comfort in gripping the stock, a recess was cut in the butt.

By the end of the second quarter of the sixteenth century the musket had evolved. More complicated forms of firing mechanisms, operated with a trigger or a bar extending back under the butt, replaced the serpentine. To drive the powder and ball firmly down into the breech, a long wooden rod, the scouring stick or ramrod, was used, which, for convenience, was housed in a recess cut into the stock beneath the barrel. Since these muskets were over five feet long and fairly heavy, musketeers could not be expected to hold them in the aiming position, and so they carried a rest, a stick of ash with a metal ferrule at one end and a U-shaped metal arm at the other.

When in action the rest was placed under the stock and served to support the weight.

Small versions of the musket were called calivers and were used without a rest. In addition to the musket and rest, the musketeer was also encumbered with horns of powder, spare lengths of match, bags of bullets and probably a sword as well. Even in the seventeenth century the infantryman needed a strong back as well as strong legs.

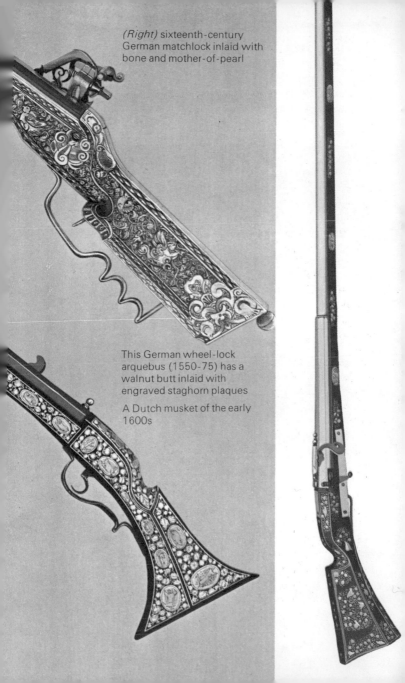

(*Right*) sixteenth-century German matchlock inlaid with bone and mother-of-pearl

This German wheel-lock arquebus (1550-75) has a walnut butt inlaid with engraved staghorn plaques

A Dutch musket of the early 1600s

Musket drill

Loading a musket was a complicated business requiring a large number of separate movements. The musketeer unhitched the slow match from the serpentine (1), then filled the pan with priming powder (2). Transferring the musket to his left hand, he pushed the cap off the charge-holder (3), poured

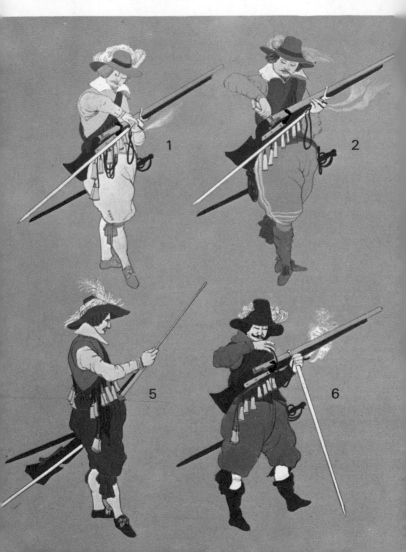

an exact measure of powder into the barrel (4) and rammed the shot home (5). One end of the burning slow match was clipped to the serpentine again (6) and the musketeer blew on it to make it glow (7). The musket was now ready for firing (8).

These pictures are based on drawings by Jakob de Gheyn, published at the Hague in 1608.

Two Italian powder flasks. *(Left)* wood flask, velvet-covered, and decorated with bronze and gilt, c. 1570. *(Right)* all-steel powder flask of the 17th century.

Apart from the musket itself the most important part of the musketeer's equipment was probably his powder container. There were two main types, each offering certain advantages. For simplicity and speed, the bandolier was probably the better. On the belt crossing the shoulder was suspended a number of horn, wood or leather-covered wood containers each holding a previously measured charge of powder sufficient for one shot.

To load was simple, for each container was opened and the charge tipped down the barrel. However, these containers could be a dangerous nuisance as the rattling could so easily betray the musketeer's presence to his enemy and, if he was not careful, a spark could ignite the powder in one container and then set off a chain explosion.

Other musketeers preferred horns to hold their powder. These were often quite simple, being made from cowhorn which had been softened by boiling. Whilst pliable, the horn was flattened and allowed to cool. The wide end was then filled by a block of wood and at the narrow end was fitted a simple but ingenious spring-operated nozzle measuring device. By placing the finger over the open end and inverting the horn whilst pressing an arm at the side of the nozzle, the musketeer made the powder run out until the nozzle was full or the cut-off was released. Most of these powder horns were decorated with simple, incised patterns or hunting scenes.

A second and smaller horn was often carried by the musketeer, containing powder of finer grain used for priming. A third type, popular during the first half of the seventeenth century, had a truncated triangular-shaped wooden body, often covered with velvet and strengthened with pierced iron plates on back, front and sides.

Less common was an annular type, frequently decorated with inlay of various materials. Most powder horns were attached to a string or strap which was slung over the shoulder or tied about the waist, but others were fitted with a belt hook so that the horn could be carried at the waist.

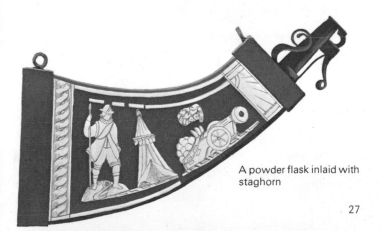

A powder flask inlaid with staghorn

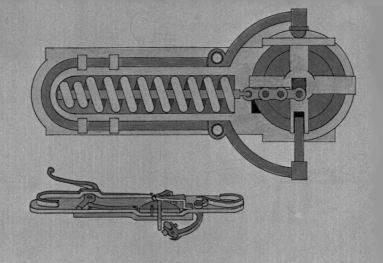

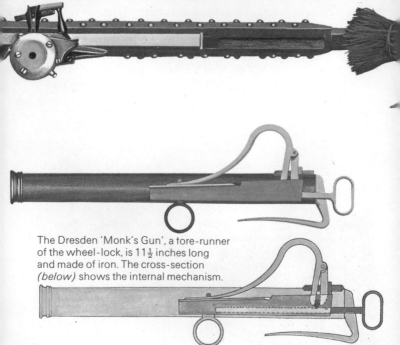

The Dresden 'Monk's Gun', a fore-runner of the wheel-lock, is $11\frac{1}{2}$ inches long and made of iron. The cross-section *(below)* shows the internal mechanism.

THE WHEEL-LOCK

Matchlocks had many disadvantages, being very much at the mercy of wind and weather, and could also betray their owners' presence. An alternative system of ignition was required, and the one that came into common use was that of producing sparks by friction between steel and a common mineral called pyrites.

In the so-called Monk's gun, power was supplied by the user who jerked the roughened bar back to make it run against the pyrites. Made, probably, at the end of the fifteenth century, the Monk's gun was one method of replacing combustion by

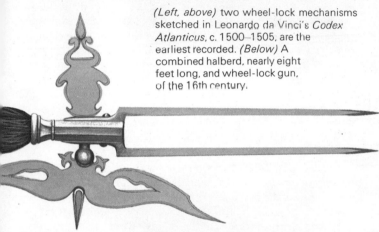

(Left, above) two wheel-lock mechanisms sketched in Leonardo da Vinci's *Codex Atlanticus*, c. 1500–1505, are the earliest recorded. *(Below)* A combined halberd, nearly eight feet long, and wheel-lock gun, of the 16th century.

friction, but more practical ones were being planned.

As early as 1500 Leonardo da Vinci made sketches of two systems using the friction principle, one of which may well have been the origin of the new system of ignition. Leonardo's plan had a steel wheel with a roughened edge which was rotated by means of a spring. As the wheel turned, the rough edge pressed against a piece of pyrites held between two jaws and so produced a stream of sparks to ignite the priming.

As early as 1507 there occur references to pistols using what was almost certainly a form of wheel-lock. The earliest surviving wheel-lock weapons date from 1510, and for the next century or so this system was to be the most widely used method of ignition.

How the wheel-lock worked

Naturally there were minor variations in the design of the wheel-lock during the period it was in use, but basically the mechanics remained unchanged. At the centre of the entire mechanism was the metal wheel with its grooved edge traversed by a series of cross cuts. The wheel was attached by a short strong chain to a large and powerful V spring.

From the hub of this wheel projected a square shank and over this fitted the square-cut end of a key which was then used to rotate the wheel and, in so doing, compress the mainspring. A small spring-activated lever, the sear, then pressed forward and engaged with a recess on the inside surface of the wheel: the lock was now spanned. The edge of the wheel protruded through the bottom of the priming pan into which the priming powder was then placed. An angular arm, the dogshead, set in front of the priming pan, was now swung forward and down until the pyrites rested on the edge of the wheel. When the trigger was pressed the retaining sear was withdrawn and the mainspring arms opened and, via the short chain, caused the wheel to rotate rapidly. Friction between the roughened edge and the pyrites produced sparks which ignited the powder and so fired the charge.

In the early wheel-locks a number of safety devices were incorporated and a distinguishing feature of these early weapons was the profusion of studs and springs visible on the plate. It was soon realized that it was far simpler to swing the dogshead clear, so removing the pyrites from contact with the wheel, and render the weapon quite safe. Wheel-lock mechanisms could be made in any size but they were complex and required skill and equipment to produce. This made them expensive and so restricted their general issue.

Germany was probably the main source of supply although many were made in Italy and France. French wheel-locks were, in fact, rather different in detail. Instead of the mainspring being attached to the lockplate, the general practice, the Gallic gunsmiths fitted the mainspring into the stock.

Princes viewed the wheel-lock with apprehension for it made the assassin's task much easier as he could now prepare the weapon and conceal it ready for instant use – something impossible with the matchlock.

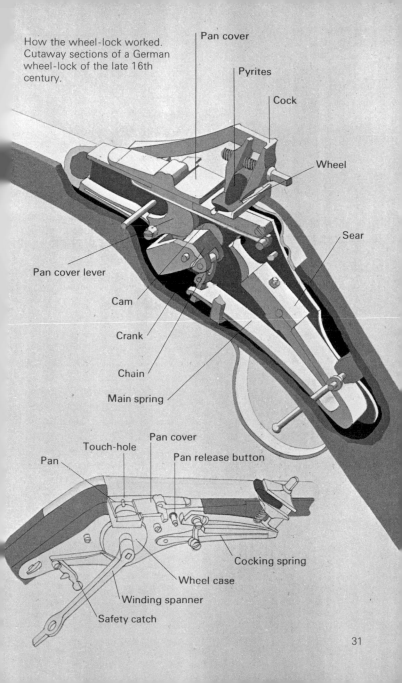

How the wheel-lock worked. Cutaway sections of a German wheel-lock of the late 16th century.

Pan cover

Pyrites

Cock

Wheel

Sear

Pan cover lever

Cam

Crank

Chain

Main spring

Pan cover

Touch-hole

Pan release button

Pan

Cocking spring

Wheel case

Winding spanner

Safety catch

31

Accessories

Like the matchlock, the wheel-lock required a certain number of accessories for its correct operation, but in general the quality of such items was much higher.

As already pointed out, the cost of a wheel-lock was considerably higher than that of a matchlock and this meant that their use was restricted to the richer groups of the community who were in a position to afford them. This group demanded higher quality workmanship and consequently the powder flasks for wheel-locks were more richly decorated and better made than most matchlock examples. In order to compress the spring and prepare the mechanism for firing – spanning the weapon – it was necessary to rotate the wheel and for this purpose a spanner or wheel-lock key was used.

Some keys were no more than bars with a square hole cut into the end which would fit over a projection from the centre of the wheel. Other, more elaborate, examples

(Top) Italian all-steel powder flask of the early 17th century, with built-in lock key and screwdriver. *(Bottom)* a combination flask, double-headed spanner and screwdriver.

were made with decorative piercing and chiselling whilst some were designed so that they could be used as screwdrivers and powder measures as well as spanners.

A few spanners were combined with powder flasks but these were less common than the normal flask. Flasks were made in a variety of forms and styles but probably the most common was that using a section of antler. A piece with a Y formation was used and two ends capped with either a wood or metal block whilst the third end was fitted with a nozzle. A spring-operated shutter, usually at the base of the nozzle, was used to control the amount of powder released.

Some of these antler powder horns were left in the natural state whilst others had one surface polished smooth and carved with a scene; hunting and classical pictures were the most popular. Other flasks were more elaborately carved and decorated. The 'doughnut' or annular style was usually embellished with inlay of good quality. The flask was sometimes fitted with a belt hook, or was worn slung from the shoulder by means of a cord or sling.

German staghorn powder flask, 1590

A copper gilt powder flask, made in Germany in 1570

Combination weapons

Whilst it was generally reliable, the wheel-lock was not without its failures. Rust could easily jam the mechanism, springs snapped and chains broke. On the other hand, it was often convenient to have a pistol in reserve should an opponent prove just a little too powerful. For one or both of these reasons gunsmiths often mounted small wheel-lock pistols on other weapons such as swords, maces, axes and even halberds. The number of such weapons surviving is fairly small so it presumably was not a common practice.

Triggers were usually set well back along the shaft and were usually in the form of a button or rod. One of the most elaborate was a sword-stick pistol. Here, an apparently ordinary stick of the seventeenth century concealed a long-bladed sword which also had a small wheel-lock pistol fired by a tiny trigger. Even stranger was a crossbow fitted with a wheel-lock. The combination seems illogical but, in fact, the earliest known wheel-lock is mounted in such a fashion.

Combined mace and wheel-lock pistol of the 16th century. Another feature is the hinged pommel cap which held charges. The weapon was suspended from the belt by a metal hook on one side of the shaft.

A flintlock carbine and battle-axe, 1690

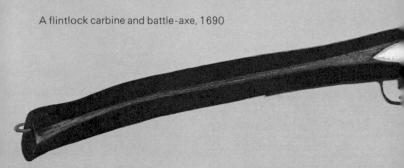

Whether it was a matter of lack of faith or simply an over-abundance of caution, some gunmakers, or perhaps it was their customers, wanted a firearm that was guaranteed to fire. Since the wheel-lock could go wrong they had a matchlock ignition system fitted in case of its failure. There was a conventional wheel-lock – although a few of these operated in the reverse direction to most, with the dogshead mounted at the butt end of the lockplate. The matchlock section was more or less standard, fitted at either end of the lockplate.

On most combination weapons there was no attempt to disguise the fact that the weapon was dual purpose, but some did have the pistol section cleverly concealed. A mace made in France around the middle of the sixteenth century has the lock completely enclosed within a raised hand guard.

It is difficult to escape the feeling that many of these combination weapons were never really intended as serious weapons but were examples of the latest idea being used whenever there was the faintest excuse so to do.

Wheel-lock pistols

For all practical purposes it had not been possible to produce matchlock pistols. The difficulties of coping with a length of glowing match were such as to make it impossible for a horseman to manage such a weapon. In some early contemporary illustrations, armoured knights on horseback are shown using handguns but experience suggests that they were few and far between.

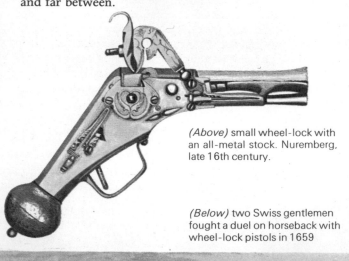

(Above) small wheel-lock with an all-metal stock. Nuremberg, late 16th century.

(Below) two Swiss gentlemen fought a duel on horseback with wheel-lock pistols in 1659

The wheel-lock changed the situation. Gunmakers could quite well construct a small lock to go into a hand firearm, and so it became possible to produce pistols. The name seems to have been derived from a town in Italy – Pistoia – though this etymology is questioned by some.

In the sixteenth century most wheel-lock pistols tended to be very elaborate and highly decorative. Many German makers favoured a stock with an acutely angled butt terminating in a large ball pommel, the whole surface being inlaid with horn, ivory or metal. The ball afforded the horseman a reasonably good means of grasping and drawing the pistol from the holster.

Another popular style of stock was almost straight, with the butt terminating in a small, six-sided oval pommel. Since the lockplate was fairly large, the stock had to be hollowed out to receive it. This naturally tended to weaken the wood and some German makers overcame the problem by building pistols with all-metal stocks. This type, naturally, tended to be plainer than those with wooden stocks.

Certain élite groups of bodyguards and cavalry units were also equipped with pistols but expense prohibited the general adoption by all troops. Those cavalry units so equipped usually carried a pair of pistols in holsters mounted in front of the saddle. Quite complicated drill patterns had to be worked out for the loading, spanning and firing of the pistol.

An over-and-under wheel-lock pistol made in Germany in 1544

Multi-barrel weapons

The greatest limitation on all early firearms was the inability to load and fire more than one shot at a time; once discharged a firearm became so much useless metal. A partial solution was to carry a pair of pistols, for this at least gave two shots but also doubled expense and weight.

Another solution was to construct the pistol with two barrels and two locks and a number of such multibarrel weapons were made. Most had the barrels mounted one above the other, each fired by a separate lock operated by its own trigger. Less common were weapons with a single lock with two wheels operated by separate pressures on the trigger.

Rather inconvenient were some made back to back, in which case the weapon had to be turned over to fire the second barrel. In all cases each barrel had to be loaded and primed and each lock spanned separately. Naturally such weapons were far more expensive than the normal wheel-lock and consequently fewer were made; no prince seems to have felt

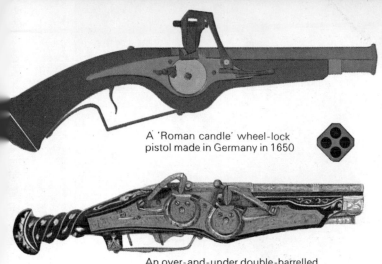

A 'Roman candle' wheel-lock
pistol made in Germany in 1650

An over-and-under double-barrelled
wheel-lock, made by the Munich gunsmith,
Peter Pech, in 1540

the need to equip an entire military unit with such weapons.

Another solution to the problem of providing more than
one shot from a single weapon was the superimposed load.
Here, one charge of powder and ball was covered with a wad
and another charge placed on top of the wad. In theory, the
charge nearest the muzzle could be fired first without affecting
the second charge which could then be fired.

One of the most spectacular systems using the superimposed
load technique was the so-called Roman candle gun. These
weapons had four barrels united into a single block. One barrel
was loaded and primed in the usual fashion whilst one of the
others was filled with powder only. The two remaining barrels
were loaded with a series of superimposed loads.

If the weapon was now fired, the first charge exploded
normally and expelled the bullet but the burst of flame was
internally diverted to the powder-filled barrel the contents of
which began to burn and act as a fuse. This barrel was connected by a series of small holes to the two barrels containing
the superimposed loads. As the powder burned down, these
charges were fired one after the other, as many as thirty in one
example, until the weapon was empty.

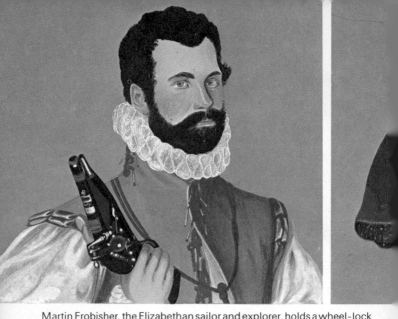

Martin Frobisher, the Elizabethan sailor and explorer, holds a wheel-lock pistol, probably English. Adapted from a contemporary portrait.

Later wheel-locks

Most of the late sixteenth century and early seventeenth century wheel-locks were made to fire a fairly small diameter ball from a very long barrel. Most were highly decorated with large ball pommels and with a variety of materials inlaid in the stock. Lockplates were large and frequently fitted with safety catches.

As the seventeenth century progressed there was a general, but no means universal, trend towards pistols with somewhat shorter barrels often firing a larger diameter ball. Lockplates were usually free of the various buttons and catches and, whereas on earlier models the wheel was plainly visible, those of the early seventeenth century were frequently covered by some form of protective cage. As the period progressed the lockplates also tended to be reduced in size.

The ornate decoration beloved by earlier gunmakers was also discarded and the trend was always towards simplicity of construction and decoration. With the plainer, more basic,

This wheel-lock pistol was made in France in 1829. One of a pair, it was probably the last wheel-lock made commercially.

type of pistol, costs were less and there was a greater use of this type of pistol although it never became a general issue weapon among military forces.

The typical military pistol of this period had a plain wooden stock and a gently down-curved butt with a slight widening at the base reinforced with a band of steel. The trigger guard, trigger and lockplate were also usually of plain steel with the wheel more or less completely enclosed.

Barrels had an octagonal breech but changed to circular section about a third of the way along their length of some fourteen inches. A slim ramrod was housed below the barrel.

By this period – mid-seventeenth century – simpler and cheaper systems of ignition were replacing the wheel-lock and soon it was abandoned for pistols, although it remained in use on long arms until the late seventeenth century.

At least one wheel-lock pistol was made after this date for there is in existence one made by the French maker, Le Page, dated 1829, but this can have been no more than a curiosity.

Hunting wheel-lock

Although wheel-lock pistols were superseded in the seventeenth century there was a continuing demand for wheel-lock hunting weapons until much later. For the rich nobleman who wanted a decorative, handsome weapon worthy of his position these wheel-lock rifles offered the solution. Most were the result of the work of half a dozen craftsmen, each a specialist. Stockmakers fashioned the body from walnut, or more exotic woods and it was then carefully cut and inlaid with ivory, staghorn or similar decorative materials.

Sometimes the inlay was in the form of plaques but more frequently it took the form of hunting or military scenes, each figure delicately engraved and set into the wood. Barrels were

The work of Hans Schmidt on the stock of a hunting wheel-lock made in 1628. It is decorated with inlaid silver wire and engraved silver plates.

thick, usually octagonal and invariably heavy. They were sometimes chiselled or inlaid with precious metal; most were rifled for greater accuracy.

To protect the butt from accidental damage should it be stood down, many had a metal ball at the very tip. Since these weapons were fired with the butt held, not against the shoulder, but to the cheek, one side was gently curved to enable an aim to be taken. Recoil was reduced by the use of

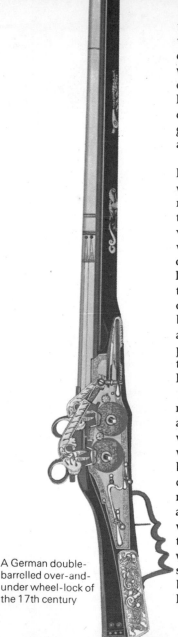

the very heavy barrel. Locks were usually decorated by chiselling and in most weapons the wheel was fitted on the inside of the plate leaving a completely flat external surface. Trigger-guards were usually large and shaped to the fingers.

To preserve the aim, most hunting weapons were fitted with hair triggers which needed but a touch to operate the mechanism. This pre-vented any tendency to wobble which a heavy pull on the trigger might well have caused. On the butt there was often a sliding bone or ivory cover held in place by a spring clip. This covered a recess which held greased patches to be wrapped around the bullet before it was loaded into the barrel.

Such rifles were still being made long after newer mech-anisms had outmoded the wheel-lock but the demand was probably sustained because of their beauty and display. Since wheel-lock mechanisms could be made in any size, many gunmakers were able to fit smaller pistols to other weapons and there were a number of maces, swords, crossbows and even a boar spear fitted with wheel-lock pistols.

A German double-barrelled over-and-under wheel-lock of the 17th century

43

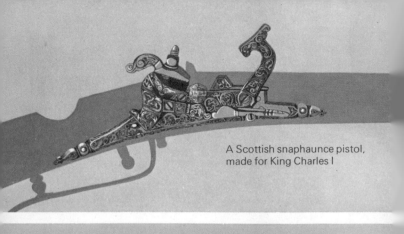

A Scottish snaphaunce pistol, made for King Charles I

The mechanism of an Italian snaphaunce lock

Cock

Battery arm

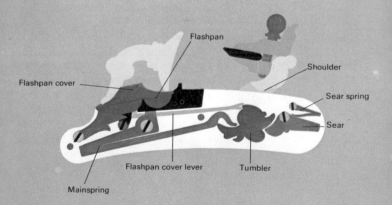

Flashpan

Flashpan cover

Shoulder

Sear spring

Sear

Flashpan cover lever

Tumbler

Mainspring

THE SNAPHAUNCE

Although the wheel-lock represented an enormous break-through in the means of igniting the charge of gunpowder, it was subject to serious limitations. The mechanism was not simple and required skill in manufacture; damage could not easily be repaired by any but a skilled armourer. Expense limited its general adoption and it was also liable to jamming.

Gunmakers naturally sought simpler and cheaper methods of achieving the same result. The same principle of striking sparks from steel and mineral was retained but in place of pyrites a more common mineral was used – flint. In place of the complicated chain, V spring and wheel systems of the wheel-lock, a much simpler arrangement comprising V spring and metal arm was substituted.

A curved arm, the cock, was fitted at the end with a pair of jaws which could be tightened around a piece of flint. This arm was pulled back, the action causing the tail of the cock to press down on the V spring. At the end of the cock's traverse a small arm, the sear, sprang out to hold the arm locked in this position. A pinch of powder was placed in the priming pan and a spring-operated lid was pushed over to cover the pan.

Another arm, pivoted on the opposite side of the pan, was fitted with a flat steel plate and when swung forward was positioned just over the covered priming pan. To fire this snaphaunce mechanism, the trigger was pressed and this withdrew the retaining arm holding the cock which, pressed by the V spring, swung forward causing the flint to slide down the face of the steel to produce sparks. Since the pan cover was opened before firing, the sparks fell into the priming and ignited the main charge via the touch hole. The force of the impact made the arm swing clear from above the pan.

The system was simple with only a minimum of moving parts to go wrong and could therefore be produced in quantity for general use in pistols or longarms. In fact, an even simpler system was produced and the snaphaunce system was never adopted on a large scale in Europe. Curiously, the system survived in North Africa until comparatively recent times. North Africans seem to have insisted on this particular mechanism and the arms factories of Liège were producing what

A 17th-century revolver with a snaphaunce lock

were in effect, copies of seventeenth-century Dutch locks until the late nineteenth century.

Snaphaunce mechanisms seem to have appeared about 1540-50. Earliest references occur in Italian records, although the name seems to have been derived from Snap Hann – Flemish for Snapping Hen, probably from the 'pecking' movement of the cock. Since the system was simple, its use spread over Europe but it was not generally adopted and snaphaunce weapons are very rare. The system was later superseded by the simpler flintlock.

The simplest form of snaphaunce lock was that known as the Baltic Lock so called because it seems to have originated in that area of Europe. The cock holding the flint was long and grace-fully curved and the toe pressed down on an external main-spring. When the cock was pulled back it was locked in position by a sear fitted on the inside of the lockplate with its nose protruding through a hole to engage with the cock. The same mainspring also served to supply tension for the arm which was fitted with the steel.

Variations on the snaphaunce evolved in the Mediterranean area and a Spanish and Italian version are recognized by collectors although the basic difference is in the manner in which the mainspring presses on the toe of the cock. Improvements in design were effected and in place of the manual opening of the pan cover an automatic system using an internal connecting lever was soon evolved. Snaphaunce weapons were quickly outmoded and the system was abandoned after a comparatively short period.

The production of snaphaunce pistols continued in northern and central Italy for some time, especially in the area around Brescia which was noted for the quality of its steel carving.

Pistols were still being produced in this area in the eighteenth century and in keeping with their tradition these Brescian gunmakers were still excelling in the quality of the chiselling and insetting of steel.

Many of the early snaphaunce actions were fitted into stocks which were originally designed for wheel-locks. A number of surviving examples have the characteristic lockplate shape of a wheel-lock with the large, semi-circular extension at the centre. Many plates were left plain but some gunmakers, like the Russians for instance, accepted the opportunities offered by the large area to carry out some extremely fine decorative chiselling thereon.

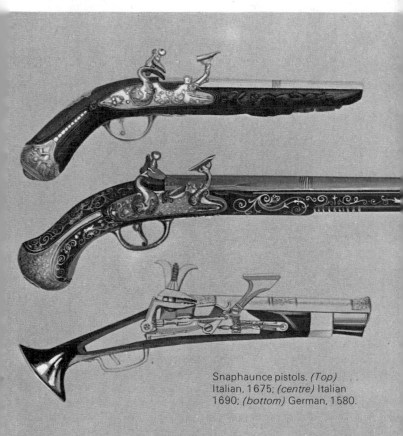

Snaphaunce pistols. *(Top)* Italian, 1675; *(centre)* Italian 1690; *(bottom)* German, 1580.

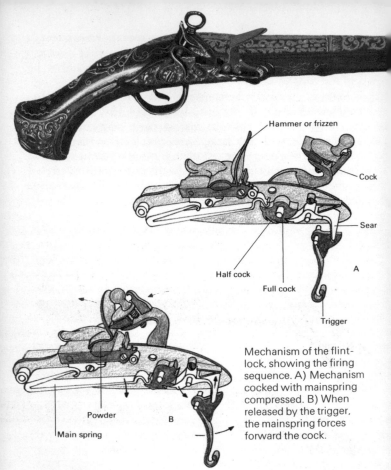

Mechanism of the flint-lock, showing the firing sequence. A) Mechanism cocked with mainspring compressed. B) When released by the trigger, the mainspring forces forward the cock.

Labels: Hammer or frizzen, Cock, Sear, Half cock, Full cock, Trigger, A, Powder, B, Main spring

THE FLINTLOCK

The snaphaunce mechanism was simple but gunmakers soon realized that it could be refined and simplified even further. As far back as the second half of the sixteenth century some gunmakers had combined the pan cover and the steel from which the sparks were struck into one single L-shaped piece of metal but the idea had not been developed. By combining the two units the action of striking sparks could also uncover the pan at the same time, for the force of the blow caused the arm to pivot.

One of a pair of Spanish flintlock pistols, made in 1760

It fell to a French gunmaker of the village of Lisieux in Normandy, Marin Le Bourgeoys, to combine two simple ideas into one unit and produce a lock mechanism which was to become more or less standard for the next two hundred years. He took the combined steel and pan cover and used that for its simplicity of action since it required less moving parts. The other feature Le Bourgeoys adopted was the use of a tumbler or metal block, situated on the inside of the lockplate and connected to the cock on the outside.

As the cock was rotated so was the tumbler, and it was on this that the mainspring pressed rather than directly against the cock. In the snaphaunce, the cock had been engaged by a metal arm, the sear, which passed through the lockplate. In the French lock the sear was fitted inside the lockplate and pressed directly on the broad edge of the tumbler. As the cock was pulled back the tumbler, pressing against the mainspring, was also rotated and the sear slid along until it engaged with a slot cut into the tumbler when it locked and so held the cock under tension. Pressure on the trigger disengaged the sear and allowed the mainspring, via the tumbler, to swing the cock forward to strike sparks from the steel. The result was a simple, reliable action.

Apart from alterations designed to make the action freer and more certain, the basic pattern was to remain unchanged until the flintlock was displaced in the early nineteenth century. To load and fire the flintlock pistol was simple. After pouring powder and ball down the barrel, a pinch of priming powder was placed in the pan. The L-shaped pan cover and steel – the frizzen – was closed and the cock pulled back until it locked. Pressing the trigger released the cock and the resulting sparks fired the charge.

This French lock soon became the universal pattern of the flintlock and was fitted to every conceivable form of firearm ranging from great wall pieces to small pocket pistols. It was to be improved over the centuries but in detail rather than principle and the basic mechanism was left unaltered.

(Above) a Dutch flintlock holster pistol, c. 1690. (Opposite) a typical Jacobean-type military flintlock such as was used by Cromwell's 'Ironsides' during the English Civil Wars.

Flintlocks were pressed into use for domestic purposes and a number of tinder lighters using this principle were made during the seventeenth and eighteenth centuries.

Many gunmakers did not produce snaphaunce weapons, progressing directly from the wheel-lock to the flintlock. This being so, it is not surprising that the shape of many early flintlock pistols closely resembled that of the wheel-lock pistols. It was not uncommon for them to retain the large bulge beneath the stock which had accommodated the wheel but was now superfluous. Gunmakers soon began to produce simpler, more graceful and slimmer stocks, often with the end of the butt swelling slightly and then cut off square.

Certain characteristics were fairly common on many of the mid-seventeenth century flintlock pistols although, naturally, there was no set pattern. Lockplates were usually flat and rather large with a plain polished surface and cocks were similar. Barrels were long, generally of octagonal section at the breech converting to circular section about a third of the way along, and fired only a small diameter bullet. The furniture, trigger guard and ramrod pipes were often fixed into position with nails rather than the screws which became general later on.

The great majority of firearms of the seventeenth century were smooth bored but a number were 'turn off' which meant that they were made so that they could be unscrewed, allowing powder and ball to be placed directly into the breech. There was obviously a danger of losing the barrel whilst loading. To prevent this a simple bar-link was fitted to join barrel to stock although allowing freedom to unscrew it.

Stocks were normally cut from walnut but some makers of the Netherlands specialized in the cutting of ivory stocks. On many of these pistols the butt terminated in a carved head. During the English Civil Wars considerable demand stimulated the growth of the British gun trade, though numbers of pistols were imported from the Continent. Many of the cavalry were still using the obsolete wheel-lock but the flint-locks were steadily beginning to dominate the market.

A few gunmakers were producing highly decorated weapons, especially in Italy where inlay was practised on a considerable scale. In London gunmakers were organized into a Gunmakers Company which claimed to control the trade.

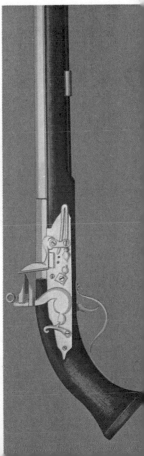

Seventeenth-century longarms

During the seventeenth century the heavy matchlock was still used by many infantry, for despite its disadvantages it was cheap to produce and maintain. However, the flintlock by virtue of its many advantages, gradually began to replace the older system and on a few surviving examples the musket has obviously been converted from the matchlock.

When the tumbler was fitted into the lock it was soon adapted to provide a safety position known as half cock. A deep notch was cut into the face, the sear engaging with this first, and movement of the trigger was insufficient to disengage it. When the cock was pulled further back, rotating the tumbler, the sear disengaged and then engaged with the shallower notch, bringing the gun to full cock. Many of the

pistols and the longarms of the seventeenth century were fitted with the dog lock.

Many English makers apparently distrusted the safety, half cock, position and fitted a hook-like arm, the dog, at the back of the lock. On the rear of the cock was a notch with which the hook engaged in the safe position. The rear of the cock was so shaped that when pulled back to the full cock position the dog was automatically disengaged.

Lockplates on longarms were generally made smaller as the century progressed but the most marked change was in the shape of the stock. The old, high comb on the butt with its deep recess cut for the thumb was gradually replaced by the simpler triangular butt, much as that used at present. In order to give support to the screws which pierced the stock to hold the lock in place, a metal strip or plate, the side plate, was also introduced. A small plate, often a shield shape, was fitted near the breech end of the butt on which could be engraved the owner's badge, initials or arms.

The huntsman *(left)* carries a flintlock fowling piece. *(Right)* a six-shot snaphaunce revolving carbine by John Dafte of London.

(Above) an English screw-barrel pistol, 11½ inches long with centrally-mounted cock, made c.1720–40. *(Below)* a screw-barrel pistol by James Freeman of London.

Eighteenth-century pistols

On most pistols the wooden stock extended to the muzzle but on others, such as the seventeenth-century rifled pistols with detachable barrels, the stock extended only half way. Since such weapons were loaded directly into the breech there was no necessity for the ramrod. This type of pistol, although not rifled, was still made in the eighteenth century though the construction was modified in a number of ways: the section containing the spring and cock were made an integral part of the barrel with the frizzen and spring on the same unit. The butt was of wood.

Pistols of this style are known by collectors as Queen Anne pistols although they were still being made long after the death of this monarch in 1714. Most are characterized by a graceful shape with a slightly swelling butt. Barrels were most often of the turn-off type which could be unscrewed, although a few were fixed and fitted with ramrods. Keys were used to unscrew the barrels. These were of two types, one of which slipped over the barrel and engaged with a lug, and the other which was pushed into the muzzle and engaged with notches cut therein.

During the first half of the eighteenth century other versions of the Queen Anne pistols were developed, including the boxlock in which the pan, frizzen and cock were mounted centrally on the breech instead of at the side.

Butts of Queen Anne pistols were often decorated with silver wire which was pressed into small grooves cut into the wood. The soft wire was then gently hammered so that it expanded and gripped the sides of the grooves. Most patterns were of the loop and whorl type although occasionally more formal designs were used. Butts were further embellished with silver escutcheon plates and butt caps usually in the form of grotesque heads. Makers usually engraved their names as well as the town of origin on the side of the breech. Pistols were frequently supplied in pairs and were certainly used in a period when highwaymen and footpads abounded.

The 18th-century gentleman 'dressed for travelling' generally included a pistol in his attire

Scottish pistols

During the seventeenth century a series of pistols with clearly recognizable characteristics developed. Among these were the Scottish or Highland pistols. Very early ones dating from the beginning of the seventeenth century were rather long with a butt which sloped only slightly and terminated in an egg-shaped pommel. Another common form, more like a fishtail with a rippled edge, was to develop into a traditional style.

Many of the pistols were made with metal stocks engraved with simple patterns. More unusual was the practice of

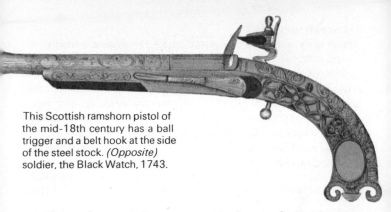

This Scottish ramshorn pistol of the mid-18th century has a ball trigger and a belt hook at the side of the steel stock. *(Opposite)* soldier, the Black Watch, 1743.

supplying these pistols in pairs with the pistols fitted with a right hand and a left hand lock. Another typical feature was the lack of a trigger guard and a ball type of trigger. Many early Scottish weapons were fitted with snaphaunce systems and it was not uncommon for the maker to engrave the date of manufacture on the pistol.

Around the middle of the seventeenth century the lobe of the butt became far more heart-shaped with two clear and distinct lobes. Later in the mid-eighteenth century there appeared the ramshorn butt in which the two ends were curled back on themselves. The custom of using metal for the stock became traditional. Most were of steel but some were made of brass. Into the base of the butt was screwed the pricker which was a pin, fitted with a large ball head, used to clean out the touch hole.

Scottish pistols were carried by members of the Highland regiments and attained great popularity after the visit of George IV to Scotland in 1822 when all things Scottish became fashionable. They soon became items of fashion rather than serious weapons and were often elaborately decorated. Most were fitted with belt hooks and carried suspended from a shoulder belt. Certain towns like Doune became renowned for their pistols in the traditional style.

Pistols of Scottish shape and design were also produced by the gunmakers of London and Birmingham. Most of those issued to Scottish Regiments were, in fact, made outside Scotland the traditional pistol being abandoned by 1795.

Spanish pistols

Spain early acquired a reputation for the high quality of her guns, and is remarkable for having retained, virtually unaltered, a style of lock, the miquelet, for three centuries. These locks are very distinctive with a squat, squarish frizzen, often with vertical grooves cut into the steel. As the mainsprings tend to be very powerful a ring is fitted to the screw to offer extra purchase when pulling the cock back.

Unlike the vast majority of flintlocks, the miquelet has the mainspring fitted on the outside of the lockplate and the spring positioned so as to operate both cock and frizzen. Miquelet locks also operate in a manner different from the usual flint-

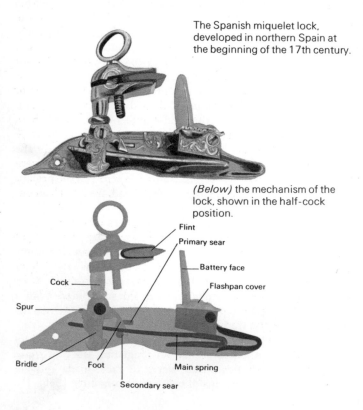

The Spanish miquelet lock, developed in northern Spain at the beginning of the 17th century.

(Below) the mechanism of the lock, shown in the half-cock position.

Flint

Primary sear

Battery face

Flashpan cover

Cock

Spur

Bridle

Foot

Main spring

Secondary sear

lock for there is no tumbler and the sears, mounted inside the lock, operate via holes in the lockplate.

As the cock is pulled back the base, which has a chisel-like arm on the front, travels through a small angle and engages with a slot cut into a spring-operated arm which protrudes through the lockplate. This is the half cock and the trigger is inoperative. But if the cock is pulled further back so that the toe disengages, another smooth sear holds it in position. Pressing the trigger will withdraw this arm allowing the mainspring which is under tension to drive the cock forward.

A type of lock which appears to be the same as other European locks is the Madrid lock but it differs from the conventional lock in the style of sear operation. A very typical Spanish type is the Ripoll pistol with its stubby appearance.

(Top) this weapon shows the characteristic shape of the Ripoll pistol. *(Below)* a 19th century miquelet pistol.

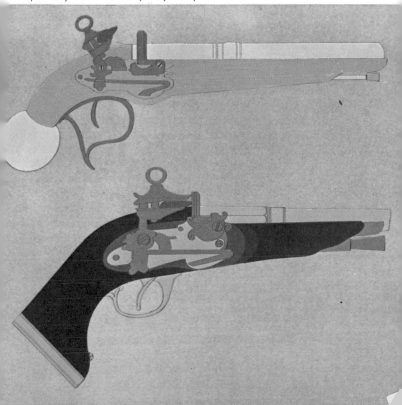

Continental flintlocks

During the Middle Ages the two main arms-producing countries were unquestionably Germany and Italy. Wheellocks were produced in quantity in Germany, Italy and France but it is interesting that, with the advent of the flintlock, both Germany and Italy declined from their previous position of arsenals for Europe and the gun trade began to develop in Britain, France and Belgium, expanding and becoming a most important industry. Italy was by no means completely eclipsed and numbers of pistols and long arms were made. In the north, around Brescia, the gunmakers excelled in the quality of their steel chiselling and delicate metal inlay work.

In Austria and Germany firearms tended to be rather heavier in general appearance although many were finely decorated. Indeed, if there is one feature which could, with some justification, serve to distinguish the Continental flintlock from the English style it is that they were far more elaborately decorated, often with carved stocks.

French firearms were of a generally high standard and particularly well decorated with a combination of several techniques. French gunmakers had long enjoyed the patronage of the monarchy and even after the revolution continued to enjoy the respect and appreciation of a generally martial government. Nicolas Boutet was one of the best-known of the French gunmakers and from his factory at Versailles came a number of decorated presentation weapons. Barrels were treated to acquire a deep and attractive blue colour whilst a pattern or motif was applied in gold. Stocks were carved or embellished with inlay and the metal work, butt caps and trigger guards were also chiselled or blued. A feature common enough to be accepted as reasonably typical of French and Belgian firearms was the pillar trigger guard. Instead of the guard being composed entirely of a flat strip the front section was in the form of a rod or pillar.

In Russia, Peter the Great established an arsenal at Tula but, in general, the Russian craftsmen tended to copy the style of French designers. The arms-producing centres of Europe, Vienna, Liège, Amsterdam and others, usually had some scheme for testing barrels before using them and those which passed the test were stamped with the town mark.

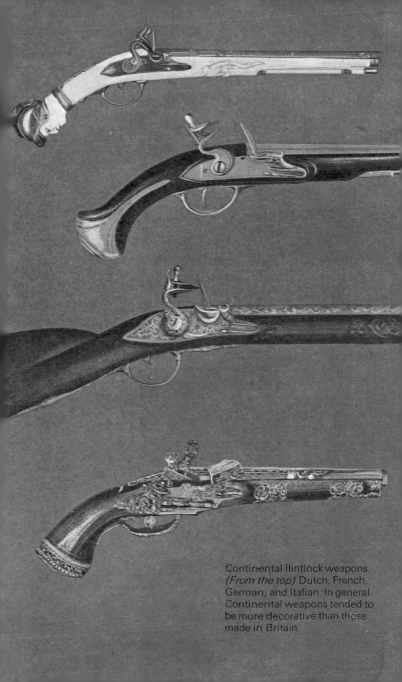

Continental flintlock weapons. *(From the top)* Dutch, French, German, and Italian. In general Continental weapons tended to be more decorative than those made in Britain.

Military weapons

Whilst a civilian might relish the thought of an elaborate and decorative weapon the prime concern of the military man was reliability. He wanted a weapon that would stand up to hard wear and still function and it is not, therefore, surprising that most military flintlocks were plain and lacking frills.

In many cases the weapons bore government and regimental markings – often the initials and perhaps a number. There was also a tendency towards conservatism in design, with one style remaining in service for many years. The only difference between weapons made twenty years apart might well be in the cypher of the monarch inscribed on the lock or barrel.

British weapons prior to 1764 bore the maker's name and a date on the lockplate but the practice was abandoned and in their place appeared a crowned G.R. and the word 'Tower'. A plain walnut stock was fitted with brass furniture and a round barrel with a wooden ramrod housed in the stock. Early in the nineteenth century a captive metal ramrod was fitted. A simple

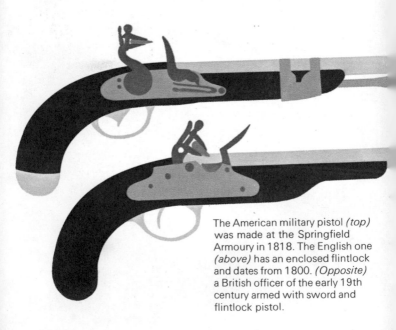

The American military pistol *(top)* was made at the Springfield Armoury in 1818. The English one *(above)* has an enclosed flintlock and dates from 1800. *(Opposite)* a British officer of the early 19th century armed with sword and flintlock pistol.

link allowed it to be used although it could not be detached from the weapon. Naval and military pistols were largely indistinguishable except that those for sea service usually had a belt hook attached.

Until the American War of Independence, 1775–1783, the vast majority of American firearms were imported from Britain but after the formation of the United States it was decided to set up arsenals. Two were founded, one at Springfield, Massachusetts and the other at Harpers Ferry, Virginia, but it was apparent from the start that their output was going to be insufficient to meet demands. Contracts were granted to civilians to supply weapons to certain specifications.

One of the most famous of these contractors was Simeon North of Connecticut. As France had been closely associated with the new nation and had supplied quantities of arms it was not surprising that North and others tended to copy the French style. Early American firearms had many points of similarity with French models. French military firearms were identified by the year of adoption and the

'Brown Bess' musket, dated 1727; this weapon remained the main arm of the British infantry for well over a century.

Americans tended to follow the same system. An arms supply system very similar to the American one was also used in Britain, most of the weapons being made in London and Birmingham.

Continental armies had largely abandoned the matchlock by the eighteenth century. In Britain early in the century there began to develop a kind of basic musket. It had a long barrel, forty-six inches, and a simple wooden stock with a wooden ramrod. The walnut stock extended the full length of the barrel except for a few inches at the muzzle to permit the attachment of a bayonet. Barrels were attached by the lug and pin method whereas the French and other Continental armies preferred a series of bands which encircled the barrel and stock. By the second quarter of the eighteenth century the famous Brown Bess musket had evolved and was established as the traditional army weapon, remaining in service, in one form or another, until the Crimean War. A steel ramrod replaced the wooden version and the barrel length was reduced from forty-six inches to forty-two inches and then later to thirty-nine inches. Why 'Brown Bess'? There is argument over the derivation of 'Brown', but 'Bess' is probably a corruption of the German – *büchse* – a gun.

Brown Bess fired a ball about three-quarters of an inch in diameter; the cavalry used smaller versions using a smaller bullet, and known as carbines. They were carried suspended from a belt slung over the shoulder and attached to the carbine by a metal clasp. Pistols carried by the cavalry fitted into holsters at the saddle. Paper cartridges fitted with powder and ball were used to load the musket and pistol.

Despite a conservative attitude, some experimenting was carried on during the latter part of the eighteenth century and early part of the nineteenth century. One result was a lock designed by a London gunmaker, Henry Nock, in which no screws at all were used, thus ensuring that it could be stripped

During the Napoleonic Wars all combatants used flintlock weapons

and reassembled with a minimum of tools and equipment. This same maker also produced seven-barrelled flintlocks for firing volleys. Most military longarms were fitted with leather slings for carrying them slung over the back.

Duelling pistols

Duelling as a means of settling a quarrel, especially one of honour, had a long history. It was even used as a means of deciding guilt. When fencing was developed, rapiers became a popular duelling weapon but their use required a degree of skill not possessed by all and soon the pistol was rivalling the sword as a duelling weapon.

At first it was just a matter of using any convenient pair of pistols but towards the end of the eighteenth century there began to develop a pistol designed exclusively for duelling. What was wanted was a pistol with a fairly short range but which was as accurate and reliable as possible and which came up to the aim with little bother.

In Britain it was not considered sporting or desirable to have rifled duelling pistols but the Continent seems not to have been as squeamish. The gunmaker made the barrel heavy to reduce the recoil and to ensure rigidity. Most were octagonal and fitted with sights and fired a fairly small diameter bullet.

It was in the design of the stock that much skill was expended, for the butt was made so that when the arm came up to fire, the pistol was on target almost without sighting. Stocks were rather hook-shaped and generally lacked all decoration except a little cross-hatching on the butt to afford a better grip. Triggers were often of the 'set' type adjusted to operate with a minimum of pressure so that there should be no going off aim as the trigger was squeezed. Trigger guards often had a long spur to afford the first finger a good grip.

These pistols were usually supplied in pairs carefully fitted into a wooden case complete with accessories such as a bullet mould, screw driver, powder flask, cleaning rods and occasionally a mallet to tap home the tight-fitting bullet.

(Opposite, top) French flintlock duelling pistols made at the beginning of the 19th century. *(Bottom)* this duel in Islington Fields, London, in 1800, ended in the deaths of both adversaries.

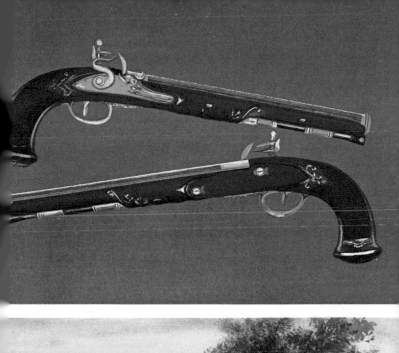

Pocket pistols

Travel in the seventeenth and eighteenth centuries was not safe either in town or in the country; even the house was not safe and it behoved a man to be prepared. When travelling in a coach or on a horse, he had no problem in carrying a pistol or even a pair, for there were holsters available. In town it was different and it was obviously inconvenient to have to carry a large pistol about. One solution was to make a small pistol that could slip into a pocket or bag and not be a nuisance. With this idea in mind gunmakers made pistols usually known as 'pocket pistols' or if very small, 'muff pistols'.

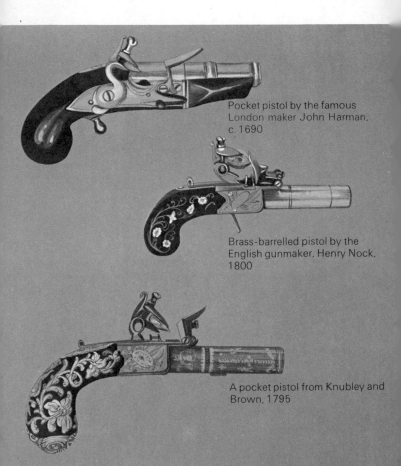

Pocket pistol by the famous London maker John Harman, c. 1690

Brass-barrelled pistol by the English gunmaker, Henry Nock, 1800

A pocket pistol from Knubley and Brown, 1795

H. Devillers of Liège made this all-metal pocket pistol. The gun, which has a silver butt, is 5·7 inches long.

The need for a small reliable pistol to fit into the pocket made the gunmaker look around for ways to ensure that it would be safe, as reliable as possible and with clean lines so that it would not snag on the inside of a pocket. Small pistols were made during the sixteenth and seventeenth centuries but it was during the eighteenth century that pocket pistols became far more common.

Most had the lock mounted centrally in the style known as a boxlock with the cock mounted centrally on the breech instead of at the side as was more normal. The frizzen and priming pan were similarly centrally mounted.

This arrangement made for ease of drawing since the size of mechanism was smaller than the conventional arrangement. It did mean that the pistol could not be aimed but since it was intended only for self defence it was unlikely to be needed for anything more than hand to hand combat. Barrels were short and to reduce still further the extras the ramrod was removed and loading was achieved by unscrewing the barrel and depositing powder and ball directly into the breech and then screwing back the barrel.

Obviously the weapon had to be carried at half cock if it was to be ready for quick action and it was therefore fitted with safety catches. Most common was the bar type which slid forward to lock the frizzen. Another type used a sliding trigger guard which locked the action at the half cock position.

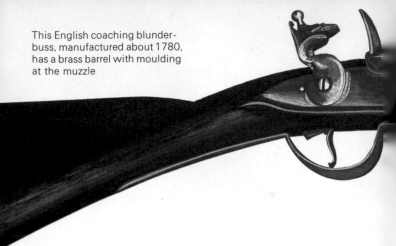

This English coaching blunderbuss, manufactured about 1780, has a brass barrel with moulding at the muzzle

The blunderbuss

One of the troubles with early firearms was that once fired they were useless. Efforts to overcome this problem were numerous and sometimes complex. Multibarrel weapons were one solution, Roman candle guns were another, and yet another was that of the single, big shot where the idea was to increase the chances of a hit with the first shot.

An obvious idea was to use a number of small balls in place of a single large ball. At close range one or two balls out of a total of twenty were very likely to hit the target. If this group of shot could be made to spread out so much the better. One way to do this was to make the barrel wider at the muzzle than the breech, an effect which could be achieved by 'belling' or opening out the walls of the barrel or, in early models, by using a parallel-sided barrel but narrowing the bore towards the breech.

Blunderbusses, as they were called, first appeared during the late sixteenth century but wheel-lock examples are very rare. The name probably derives from *donder büchse* – thunder gun – and certainly the wide muzzle amplified the roar of the explosion. Experiments have clearly indicated that the spread of the shot is affected only to a limited extent by the belling of the barrel.

Blunderbusses were popular as personal protection weapons from the seventeenth century to the early nineteenth when

the revolver replaced them. Most blunderbusses were flint-lock and comparatively few percussion models were made.

Blunderbusses were carried by the guards of Royal Mail coaches and a number were issued to military and naval units. Barrels were of brass or steel and, in the case of Indian ones, were often of steel with brass decoration. A few pistols were also produced with the flaring barrels but they seem to have been less popular than the larger weapon.

Despite popular belief, they were seldom, if ever, loaded with nails and odd pieces of old iron but rather with twenty or so small lead bullets. Here, the funnel-shaped barrels must have facilitated loading.

A shot from a blunderbuss killed Thomas Thynne in a notorious 17th-century plot. He was murdered so that his wife might elope with the Count of Königsmark.

Spring bayonet weapons

The greatest moments of danger for the musketeer had been whilst he was reloading, for then he was defenceless. In the seventeenth century groups of pikemen had been mixed in with the musketeers to hold off any attacks. Their sixteen- to twenty-foot long pikes with stout ash staves and long steel points were effective but clumsy. During the century there developed a simple device which converted the empty gun into a short pike, rendering the pikeman unnecessary.

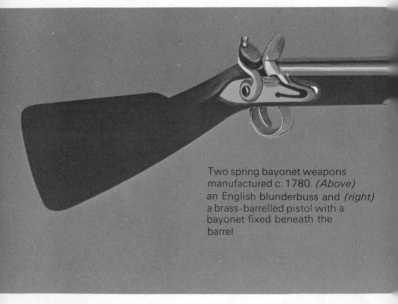

Two spring bayonet weapons manufactured c. 1780. *(Above)* an English blunderbuss and *(right)* a brass-barrelled pistol with a bayonet fixed beneath the barrel

Bayonne, in France, was famous for its production of knives and it was this town which gave its name to the bayonet. Traditionally this weapon was first used when a group of fighters with empty muskets pushed the hilts of their knives into the muzzles. This simple and obvious innovation converted the musket into a short spear useful for holding off an enemy. Early examples were called plug bayonets and had a simple, tapering wooden grip and a plain cross guard. Blades were fairly short and broad at the base but tapered to the point.

Obviously plug bayonets were of limited value since they rendered the musket completely useless and it was not long before more satisfactory methods of fixing were devised. One such was a socket, or tube-like attachment fitted at the end of a triangular bayonet. This slipped over the outside of the muzzle, being held in place by a slot fitting. In the middle of the nineteenth century a more efficient system using a spring clip and lug fitting was adopted. Despite the attitude of many militarists the bayonet was not a good offensive weapon.

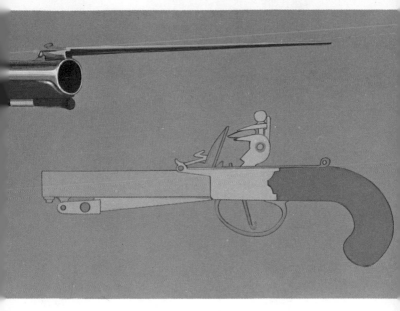

Although the bayonet was of questionable value for personal or coach defence, many blunderbusses and pistols were made with a bayonet permanently attached to the barrel. The blade was folded back along the barrel and held down by a catch. When this was released a spring forced the blade to swing into place and lock. A catch had to be pressed to release the bayonet when it was no longer needed. A British patent on the idea was taken out by John Waters in 1781 and weapons with this fitting were fairly common about this period.

A richly-ornamented combination sword and wheel-lock pistol, mid-16th century

Pistol swords

Spring bayonets were an addition to a firearm – the prime weapon; but in some cases a pistol was fitted as a secondary weapon, usually to a sword. Wheel-lock pistols were fitted to swords but it was with the adoption of the flintlock that such pistol swords became a little more common. Many were of the hunting type and were presumably intended to dispatch a wounded prey with a coup de grâce.

However, a number of pistols were fitted to military-type swords, so presumably they were intended as a serious weapon to be used in self-defence or attack. Percussion versions of these pistol swords were made but not in such large numbers as for the flintlock. There were even a few patented for use with cartridge weapons. As many as four barrels were fitted to a few such weapons but the majority had only a single barrel.

Most of the examples of this type of weapon had a fairly short blade with the pistol mounted on the side of the blade, just below the grip. The trigger was normally set into the grip and was just behind the quillon or

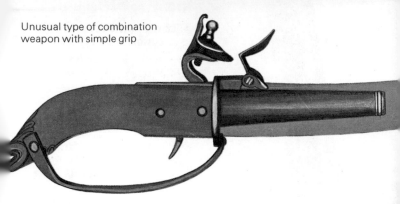

Unusual type of combination
weapon with simple grip

guard. Barrels were short and the entire mechanism was robust rather than decorative. Barrels unscrewed for reloading and this rendered the ramrod superfluous.

A rarer type comprised a pistol fitted with a sword blade. In this weapon the butt of the pistol formed the grip of the sword. With the advent of the percussion system a number of pistol knives were made. These were essentially a penknife with a small bore pistol built in.

How effective any of the combined sword and pistol weapons were is open to discussion but certainly there are few, if any, references in contemporary material to their use, successful or otherwise. Apart from later odd and rather outrageous devices, the pistol sword had had its day by the early nineteenth century.

An English combined sword and pistol of the mid-18th century

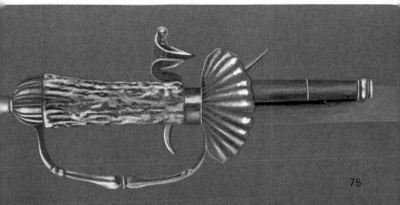

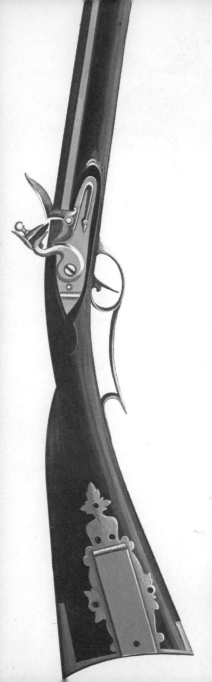

The Pennsylvania rifle

Accurate shooting depended on many factors some of which could be controlled and others which could not. Rifling was obviously a basic necessity but if the barrel was long this further increased the accuracy. Heavy barrels reduced the recoil and so contributed towards greater accuracy.

The length of a barrel also had an effect and, all things being equal, a longer barrel made for better shooting as did smaller bore bullets. Wheel-lock rifles were expensive but accurate, so many European makers copied the basic design using the flintlock mechanism but incorporating many of the wheel-lock

features, such as heavy rifled barrels and small bore. Such Jaeger rifles became quite popular in Europe.

Among the Germanic immigrants to the New World were gunsmiths who took with them their skills and methods of firearms manufacture. When they settled and began production they copied their old Jaeger rifle, though adapting their style. In Europe stocks had been made of walnut, a wood not plentiful in the USA, so maple was often substituted.

A new style of gracefully downcurving butt evolved, with a deep curve to fit snugly around the shoulder. Barrels were long, usually octagonal and with thick walls to give weight which would reduce the recoil and improve accuracy. Furniture was usually of brass.

Set in the butt was a rather ornate brass lid which covered a recessed patch box holding greased linen patches to wrap around the bullet before it was pressed home into the barrel. This style of long rifle came to be known as the Kentucky rifle, although it was produced mainly in Pennsylvania.

All these features combined to make the Pennsylvanian long rifle famed for its accuracy and it remained popular until

The Pennsylvania rifle *(opposite)*, long known as the Kentucky rifle, was America's first great contribution to fire-arm manufacture.

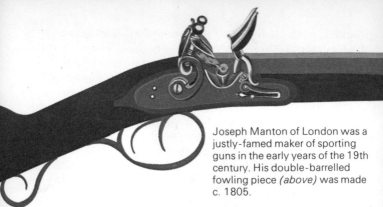

Joseph Manton of London was a justly-famed maker of sporting guns in the early years of the 19th century. His double-barrelled fowling piece *(above)* was made c. 1805.

the mid-nineteenth century when newer types of weapons rendered it obsolete. During its working life it saw service in the American War of Independence as well as the War of 1812.

Sporting guns

Hunting has always been either a matter of necessity or a pastime for those with leisure. For those to whom it was a necessity the weapon was largely incidental, and as long as it fired with reasonable accuracy its appearance was of secondary importance.

Those who regarded hunting as a pleasant way to pass the time were usually wealthy and tended to regard the gun as something more than a tool; they wanted every refinement and decoration. There were long debates on the best type of barrel, the correct charge of powder, type of wadding and amount of shot. Considerable sums of money were spent on acquiring true and accurate shooting barrels.

Before the eighteenth century most of London's gunmakers were located in the area around the Tower of London but gradually they set up in the newer and more fashionable parts of London. Their names were soon known to all shooters. Often there were several makers of the same family like the Eggs, Mantons, Nocks and others. Many introduced patented ideas such as waterproof pans and sundry safety devices and features to improve the performance of their products. Touch holes and pans were lined with gold or platinum, metals which resisted the fouling, corroding effect of the burning powder.

English stocks tended to be rather plain, with perhaps a little hatching at the small of the butt to afford a firmer grip and a simple scroll or two along the grip. On the Continent there was a far greater use of carving. Sometimes the butt was fashioned into a restrained, but grotesque head, and the rest of the stock was perhaps covered with tracery.

On many of the British weapons, one of the most pleasant features was the colour and pattern on the barrel. To afford greater strength, the metal used for barrels was fashioned from layers of iron and steel folded and wrapped over one another. This resulted in a varying pattern on the surface of the metal which was emphasized when the metal was chemically treated to form a brownish, rust-resisting skin.

From the middle of the 18th century shooting at flying, rather than sitting, birds became popular and for this guns had to be accurate

Powder flasks and testers

Powder flasks were used throughout the sixteenth century, but during the seventeenth century there was a gradual change over to cartridges for military purposes. The first cartridges were paper packets holding the correct charge of powder which were torn open and the powder poured down the barrel to be followed by the ball.

By the end of the sixteenth century it was becoming more usual to combine powder and ball inside one packet. By the early eighteenth century most soldiers carried a bag or box holding a number of these ready-made paper cartridges. Later, in place of loose cartridges, a wooden block drilled with a number of holes, each holding a single cartridge, was adopted.

Paper cartridges were in service until well into the nineteenth century although other materials were also used.

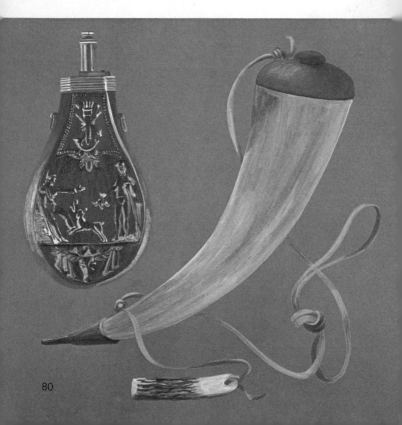

Although military usage was towards the cartridge, in sporting circles the flask was still popular. Sportsmen felt that for accurate shooting it was essential to measure out each individual charge and therefore they retained the flask in one form or another. Easiest to make was the horn which had one end sealed by a wooden block and the pointed end fitted with a spring-operated pourer.

Sportsmen eschewed such crudities, preferring pear-shaped copper flasks which could be either plain or embossed with scenes. Most had a nozzle which could be set to give a number of measures of powder. On a few flasks the nozzle was made to pivot so that any odd sparks could only ignite one charge of powder instead of the whole flask. Flasks were also made to hold the lead shot used for the loading of the guns. Shot flasks were often of leather with a metal nozzle fitted with an ingenious double cut-off.

The French infrantryman's cartridge pouch *(right)* comprises a main pouch, large flask, touch-hole pricker (on chain), small flask and bayonet. *(Opposite page)* a French embossed copper powder flask, c. 1830, and a powder horn with a small stag-horn measuring cup.

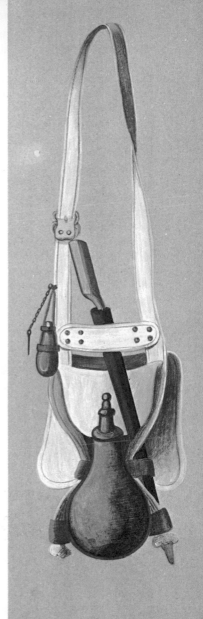

Gunpowder is a mixture of three substances – saltpetre (potassium nitrate), charcoal and sulphur, but the number of variant mixtures of these three compounds is considerable. Bacon proposed a ratio of approximately seven parts of saltpetre to five each of sulphur and charcoal. German powder of the fourteenth century was four of saltpetre to six equal parts of charcoal and sulphur. By the late eighteenth century English powder was standardized in the ratio of seventy-five parts of saltpetre to fifteen of charcoal and ten of sulphur.

Obviously, the variation of component quantities would alter the explosive quality of the powder. When the mixture was simply one of powders the components tended to separate with shaking so that within the same barrel there could be quite appreciable variations in samples taken from the top and the bottom. Early powder also had the unfortunate quality of absorbing water from the air, which again affected its performance. Improved methods of production resulted in a more consistent product but even so if any accurate shooting was to be done it was important to have some idea as to the explosive qualities of the powder.

There could be no absolute standards, but rather a comparative reading, and to obtain such readings powder-testers were used. These all worked on basically the same principle –

(Right and opposite, below) two late 18th-century English powder testers

that of pushing against a fixed weight.

Powder testers were made to operate with all forms of ignition, but most consisted of a small chamber which held a tiny charge of powder. This chamber was covered by a spring-tensioned lid which, when the powder was ignited, was forced open by the explosion and held open by some form of retaining arm or spring. On the arm was a set of figures.

The terminating position of the arm gave some form of reading which, after test firing, could be used as a standard against which other charges might be compared and adjustments in charge or aiming made.

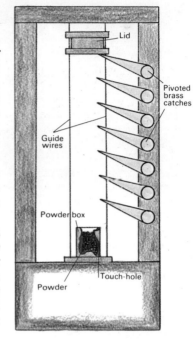

(Above) this box powder tester worked on the same principle as the two below, except that the ignited powder, instead of pushing a wheel around, lifted a weight (the lid) up two guide wires

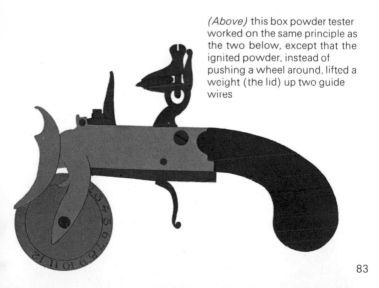

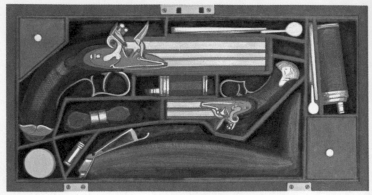

A pair of multi-barrelled pistols in their specially-made case

Multi-shot weapons

The blunderbuss was one method of increasing the chances of securing a hit with a single discharge, relying on the spread of several projectiles. An alternative approach was to use one firearm with several barrels, each being discharged separately.

Multibarrel weapons had been produced from the very beginning and multibarrel handguns were apparently used in numbers; matchlock examples were still being made in India in the nineteenth century. With the adoption of the wheel-lock, such weapons were usually limited to two barrels mounted one above the other – the over and under system.

It was with the use of the flintlock that multibarrel weapons, usually pistols, became a little more common.

During the later part of the eighteenth century the most usual type was the tap action pocket pistol. Both barrels were loaded and then the lower one was primed by placing some powder in a recess in the centrally mounted boxlock. As an arm mounted on the outside of the breech rotated, the block, recessed to hold the priming for the lower barrel, was also turned. The edge of the block now formed the base of the priming pan for the top barrel which was now primed and fired normally. If the arm was now turned back it exposed the ready primed recess which was connected by a small channel to the lower barrel; the frizzen was now closed and the pistol was ready for the second shot to be fired.

A few pistols, known as duck's foot pistols, were made with four barrels arranged in a fan shape. These were intended for use in confined spaces against mobs and all the barrels were fired simultaneously.

Very similar were the seven-barrelled volley guns used by the Royal Navy as an effective weapon for sweeping a deck or the fighting tops of an enemy ship. Each of the barrels was loaded in the usual style but the priming was connected by a touch hole to the central barrel only. When this barrel was fired the flash was transferred by a small connecting hole to the other barrels arranged concentrically about the centre.

A few of these volley guns were made with as many as twelve to fourteen barrels but their weight was excessive and their benefits marginal so that they were not developed to any large extent.

One of the greatest problems in making an efficient repeating weapon using a multi-shot cylinder, was that of accurately

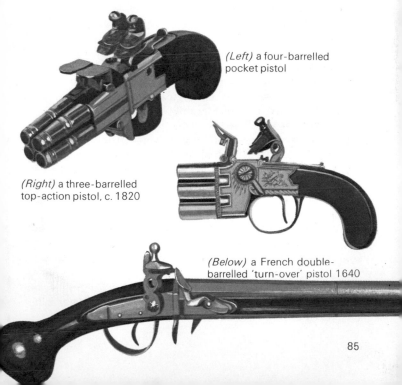

(Left) a four-barrelled pocket pistol

(Right) a three-barrelled top-action pistol, c. 1820

(Below) a French double-barrelled 'turn-over' pistol 1640

lining up each charge in the cylinder with the barrel. If there was an appreciable gap between barrel and cylinder, the loss of power was considerable and shooting suffered accordingly.

There were many attempts to overcome this, some of which were quite efficient. Undoubtedly one of the most unusual was the Puckle machine gun which was, in many ways, far ahead of its time. It was a very efficient weapon, for it is recorded that in 1722 during a rainstorm, it fired sixty-three shots in seven minutes. In spite of this incredible performance the weapon was not exploited by the military and it disappeared from the scene.

It was the brain child of a London notary, James Puckle, who obtained a patent in May 1718 for a 'Portable gun or machine called a defence'. A single barrel, between two-and-a-half and three feet long, was fitted on a tripod and with this went a series of cylinders each holding up to eleven chambers.

The bullets were about one inch in diameter and an intriguing choice of ammunition was offered. For Christian foes conventional round bullets were available but an added inducement were the special cylinders for shooting square bullets against the Turks. Puckle formed a company to manufacture and exploit his amazing gun but surprisingly he had little or no success. Fundamentally the design was quite practical and he overcame the very serious leakage and loss of power inherent in revolver design by a simple, but efficient, arrangement. As each chamber of the cylinder came opposite the barrel, the cylinder was screwed up tight against the breech which was tapered to sit snugly just inside the chamber, so ensuring a good tight seal. As each cylinder was emptied, another, pre-loaded, could be fitted and so maintain a continuous rate of fire.

Ignition was planned to be either by match or by flintlock; of the three known surviving examples only one is flintlock. Two are made of brass and one is of iron. Although the details of the rest are on record, there is no indication that they were ever fired in anger although two went with the Royal Navy for service in the West Indies.

Interest in machine guns lapsed and no further serious attempts are recorded until the American Civil War when Gatling produced his famous model.

The Puckle Gun *(above)*, fired by a flintlock mechanism, had alternative cylindrical magazines *(right)*. one for firing round bullets at Christians, the other for square bullets to be used against Turks

(Right) a single magazine showing its vent and cover

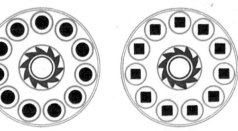

The Rev. Alexander John Forsyth, 1769–1843, was a Church of Scotland clergyman

This double-barrelled fowling piece, made c. 1820, has locks fitted with swivel, Forsyth scent-bottle primers. The overall length of this gun is 46 inches, the barrel being 30 inches long.

THE PERCUSSION GUN

Flintlock systems worked well and were generally satisfactory but they were not without their drawbacks. Misfires were not infrequent, and for the targetshooter and hunter there was a greater limitation – the hangfire. From the moment when the trigger was pressed to the explosion there was a small, but appreciable, delay as cock swung forward, priming ignited and the flash passed through the touch hole.

What was needed was a quicker, simpler, more consistent

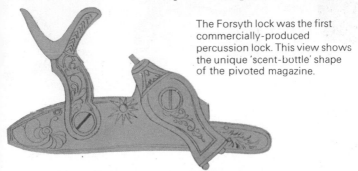

The Forsyth lock was the first commercially-produced percussion lock. This view shows the unique 'scent-bottle' shape of the pivoted magazine.

means of ignition and the answer came from Scotland. The Reverend Alexander Forsyth was the minister at Belhelvie in Aberdeenshire, Scotland and was blessed with an active, enquiring mind as well as a passion for shooting.

He was particularly bothered by the hangfire problem. As a result of his interest in matters chemical he was familiar with the explosive qualities of a group of unstable chemical compounds known as fulminates.

Knowing that crystals of this group of chemicals would explode on impact, Forsyth reasoned that the flash produced by such a minor explosion could be used to trigger off a larger explosion. He sought means of depositing a few grains of fulminate in the touch hole of a gun and then exploding it by impact. He produced his famous 'scent bottle' which did just this and in 1807 patented his system.

Although he pointed the way to a more efficient system Forsyth did not greatly benefit from his discovery and he returned to Scotland after spending some time in London, during which he worked for a while at the Tower of London.

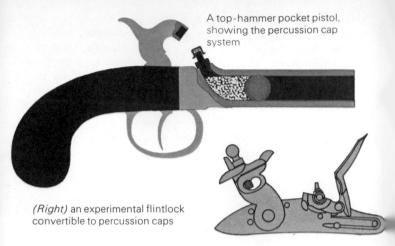

A top-hammer pocket pistol, showing the percussion cap system

(Right) an experimental flintlock convertible to percussion caps

Percussion locks

Forsyth had pointed the way and soon others were experimenting with the idea. His scent bottle had been a delicate piece of mechanism which was not really suitable for rough usage. Gun designers sought other ways of placing the fulminate easily, quickly and safely in position.

A variety of systems appeared on the market; fulminate-packed tubes, pills and discs were produced for the new detonating locks which were essentially simpler in construction than the flintlock. Pills of fulminate were fashioned using binding material such as wax but the low melting point caused problems.

Dr Guthrie, an American, conceived the idea of using a gum arabic base. His system consisted of placing the pills in a shallow depression over the touch hole and allowing the hammer, which was fitted with a sharp point, to strike the pill. In England, Joseph Manton patented a very similar idea but his pills were fitted on the head of the hammer.

All these pills suffered from the common drawback of size for they were difficult to handle at the best of times but in the field or in bad weather it was almost impossible for the user to cope with them.

To overcome the problem of size some gunmakers fitted the fulminate capsules into the centre of discs of paper, card or thin metal and then coated them with wax. Others placed the pills of fulminate into tiny tubes of metal or thin quill ends which were slipped into some form of retainer fitted over the touch hole. The head of the hammer was fitted with a knife-like edge which came down to strike the thin tube.

A few weapons were fashioned with tape priming in which a series of pills were fixed to a continuous, narrow strip of paper in exactly the same way as a present day child's roll of caps. Tape priming was a useful device and coupled with the use of paper cartridges enabled a rapid rate of fire since the action of priming was now obviated.

Although these systems were all quite practical each had some weakness and it soon became apparent that the most satisfactory was the copper percussion cap. These were com-

Tube primers   Metal percussion caps   Paper-wrapped
                                                      packet containing
                                                      twelve percussion
                                                      cartridges

A duelling pistol by Durs Egg, converted to use of percussion caps

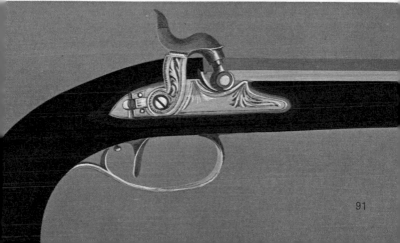

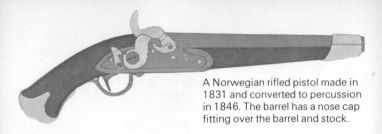

A Norwegian rifled pistol made in 1831 and converted to percussion in 1846. The barrel has a nose cap fitting over the barrel and stock.

paratively simple to manufacture, extremely safe in use and very reliable. Their advantages were so great as to ensure that they were soon universally adopted, ousting almost all other systems then being used.

There were so many claimants for the honour of being the first to invent the copper percussion cap. General opinion accepts Joshua Shaw as the candidate with the most impressive case. Shaw was a landscape painter who emigrated from Britain to the USA. He claimed that he was using a cap as early as 1815 although he did not apply for a patent until 1822. Shaw's cap, in its final form, comprised a short, closed copper tube with a small amount of fulminate deposited on the inside of the closed end.

The copper percussion cap was very convenient for it was reasonably safe and not so small that it could not be handled with comparative ease. Many flintlock weapons were converted to the new percussion system, a relatively simple matter for the gunmaker.

Most conversions used a pillar and drum system in which the touch hole was drilled out and a small metal drum inserted. Fitting into this drum, at a slight angle, was a thin pillar, the nipple, which was drilled with a tiny hole running through to the drum and then on to the touch hole. The frizzen and spring were removed from the lock plate and in place of the cock a hammer was fitted which struck down on the cap which was push-fitted over the top of the nipple.

In the interest of safety the cap was made of thin ribbed copper so that it split easily. To stop pieces flying, the nose of the hammer was recessed to fit well over the nipple and so contain the pieces.

Many shooters preferred their old tube and pill locks but the vast majority of new weapons produced were made with

Contestants using percussion target rifles in a turkey shoot

the cap system. Birmingham and Liège, for example, produced large numbers of cheap, single shot, pocket pistols using percussion caps as well as sporting guns of inferior quality.

Military men were less quick to take up the new system and it was not until 1838 that the British Army officially adopted the system after due and cautious consideration.

Percussion caps offered a far more certain means of ignition and comparative tests with the flintlock showed a much lower percentage of misfires. Weather, wind and rain were far less liable to affect the cap compared with the hazards of damp priming powder or pans emptied by a gust of wind.

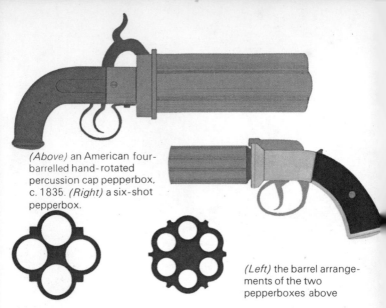

(Above) an American four-barrelled hand-rotated percussion cap pepperbox, c. 1835. (Right) a six-shot pepperbox.

(Left) the barrel arrangements of the two pepperboxes above

The pepperbox

The new copper percussion cap made lock construction very much simpler, especially in the field of repeating weapons, for moving frizzens were no longer required. Flintlock revolvers had been designed and made by various makers but they were, in general, a little too complex and involved for general use.

Copper percussion caps completely altered this situation and during the second quarter of the nineteenth century there appeared the first of the simple revolvers – the pepperbox.

A solid block of metal was drilled with five or six barrels arranged concentrically around the axis. Each barrel had a separate nipple and was loaded and capped individually. The cap was impacted by a hammer which was either conventionally shaped or, more simply, a flat bar with a small drum end.

Pepperboxes were apparently produced in quantity for they were extremely good for personal defence. A few longarms of of the same design were made but the rather excessive weight made them impractical.

On some pepperboxes the barrel block had to be rotated by hand but on most the action of pulling back the trigger caused the block to rotate to line up the next unfired barrel ready for

Pepperbox made by Parkhouse of
Taunton together with a wad
cutter, bullet mould and nipple key

the cap to be struck by the hammer. These pepperboxes were
not very accurate but as they were intended for self-defence
weapons, to be used only at close quarters, poor accuracy did
not greatly matter.

The pepperbox was often sold in a wooden, baize-lined case
in which compartments held a variety of necessary accessories
such as powder flask, bullet mould for casting the bullets, a
screwdriver and, since none was attached to the pistol, a
ramrod. This might be a separate item or it could be part of the
bullet mould.

The large barrel block made these weapons rather top heavy
and many gunsmiths produced instead what is known as the
transitional revolver. In place of five or six separate barrels
one common barrel was fitted whilst the cylinder was greatly
reduced in length. Many of the better quality examples were
made with a simple arrangement that made the cylinder sit
very snugly over the end of the barrel.

It is interesting to note that the pepperbox was one of the
first firearms to be carried in a holster slung on the belt. Their
design was inferior to Colt's revolvers but continued in production long after his patent was granted.

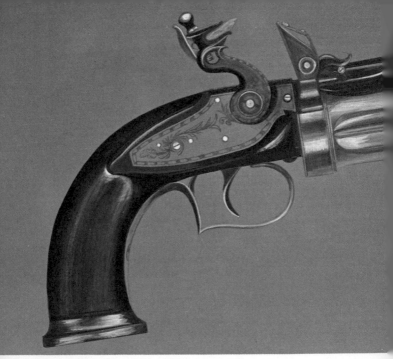

A Collier flintlock revolver, made about 1820

Revolvers

Pepperboxes and transition revolvers were both useful weapons but still not ideal. Revolvers had been designed by such men as Elisha Collier, an American who was granted a British patent in 1818. Collier's revolver had a cylinder holding the charges and bullets and a single barrel. Its most unusual feature was a clockwork mechanism which caused the cylinder to rotate and which had to be wound up before use. Collier seemed to find the system unsatisfactory for he discarded it.

Like Puckle before him, Collier ensured a good fit by using a slightly recessed mouth to each chamber and a slightly tapered end to the barrel. A spring applied pressure to the cylinder to ensure close contact. Collier's revolvers were fitted with a self-priming pan cover which operated as it was closed after each shot. Even with all these refinements flintlock revolvers were not really reliable.

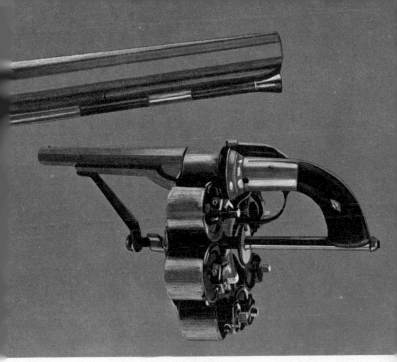

This multiple-cylinder revolver by Joseph Enovy was patented in 1855

Percussion pepperboxes represented a step forward but they had their limitations for they were heavy and cumbersome. They also had an unfortunate tendency to go into a Roman Candle effect when one cap, in firing, would ignite the rest. Accuracy was low, for the barrels were smooth bore, as rifling five or six chambers was rather too great a technical problem and too costly for the type of weapon.

The transition revolver offered an improved accuracy as the single barrel was usually made with micro-rifling. Many of the better quality weapons were fitted with the slight reciprocating movement of the cylinder to improve cylinder and barrel seal. One oddity had a whole series of cylinders mounted on an arm.

However, unknown to most of the makers of the period, the pepperbox was obsolete from the time it was first used, for a true, efficient revolver was on its way.

Samuel Colt's revolver

It was an American who first came up with a simple, practical and efficient revolver, though his product was not appreciated at once and he came close to complete bankruptcy.

Samuel Colt was born in Hartford, Connecticut in 1814 and spent his youth in a variety of occupations that were, in fact, to prove valuable in later life. In 1830 he sailed as a midshipman on board a brig and tradition has it that during the voyage he whittled a wooden model of the mechanism that was to make the revolver a practical weapon. Upon his return to the United States he drew up official drawings and diagrams and in 1835–6 obtained patents for his revolver action in Britain and America.

The action was simple and positive and he soon attracted enough capital to start the Patent Arms Manufacturing Company of Paterson, New Jersey. Despite the obvious advantages of these new weapons the US Army and the general market evinced little enthusiasm and orders were few and far between. Within three years the company ceased trading. However, enough examples of these early Paterson Colts were in circulation for their values to be recognized and in 1847 Colt was once again in production making large revolvers for the Mexican War.

From then on his factories flourished. The range of models grew and thanks to Colt's flair for publicity demand also grew.

Samuel Colt, father of the modern revolver

United States troops were the first in the world to be issued with revolvers. They used the Walker Colt *(above)* in 1847.

Colt's action was simple: as the hammer was pulled back with the thumb the cylinder was rotated and, at the full cock position, locked in position; pressure on the trigger now released the hammer which flew forward to strike the cap set on a nipple. Butts, usually walnut, had a typical shape.

The cylinders were engraved with a set scene. The Dragoon models showed a running fight with Indians; the smaller pocket-pistol showed a stage-coach hold-up whilst the Navy Colt showed ships in battle. Some Belgian-made models had a great variety of other motifs engraved on the cylinders.

Many of Colt's revolvers were sold cased complete with accessories. Such sets are now highly prized. Another of Colt's innovations was the principle of interchangeability by which means it was possible to replace any component of a particular model directly from stock.

'When Guns Speak, Death Settles Dispute'. This picture is based on a painting by Charles Russell.

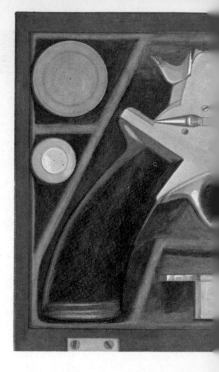

Robert Adams *(above)* provided a serious rival to Colt's gun when he patented his double-action revolver in England in 1851. *(Right)* the Adams revolver.

The Adams revolver

Because of interest shown at the 1851 Great Exhibition in London, Samuel Colt was persuaded that demand was sufficient to justify the setting up of a factory in London. He was regarded by British gunmakers as an interfering American with no right to assail the home market and he met with considerable opposition.

Much of the comment was unjustified for his revolvers were superior to any British equivalent in the early days. However, a number of revolvers were now being produced which were worthy rivals of the American model.

Probably the best known were those made by Robert Adams, who had patented a five-shot, self-cocking revolver in 1851. At this period Colt was producing quantities of the Navy Colt and this weapon was compared with the Adams. Each had supporters who swore that one or the other was infinitely superior. One of the greatest differences lay in the

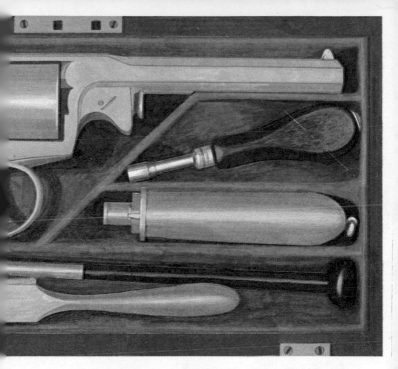

mechanical action. Colt's revolver had to be cocked between each shot – the hammer was pulled back and this action rotated the cylinder.

Adams revolvers were self-cocking which meant that pressure on the trigger caused the cylinder to rotate, the hammer to cock and, if the pressure continued, allowed the hammer to fall and the weapon to fire.

Single-action was said to be economical and better for careful shooting whereas double-action made for faster shooting – a vital consideration in war. Adams revolvers, superbly made, were fitted with a characteristic butt with a spur at the top of the grip. Early Adams had no attached loading levers.

In 1855 Lt F. Beaumont patented a mechanism which could be used both as self-cocking or manually cocked by the thumb. Adams revolvers were popular and many were produced in London and Birmingham. Numbers were imported by both sides during the American Civil War.

The Tranter revolver

Another British gunmaker whose name came to the fore during the second half of the nineteenth century was William Tranter. At first he manufactured revolvers for Adams at his establishment in Birmingham, but in 1853 he patented an idea for an improved version of the Adams revolver which incorporated a fairly novel idea: a double trigger.

In general appearance the Tranter revolver was conventional but the trigger was long, double-curved and projected down through the guard. If this long trigger was pressed by the second finger the cylinder was rotated and the action cocked but it did not fire the weapon. To fire, the first finger activated a small trigger set inside the section of trigger contained within the space of the trigger guard.

By this method it was possible to bring the revolver up to the firing position cocked and to hold this position to aim or check the target until ready to fire when a comparatively light pressure was all that was needed. If pressure was applied simultaneously to both triggers the weapon functioned like a conventional double-action revolver, so allowing rapid fire.

Early examples of the double-trigger revolver had no attached loading lever but since the separate ones were probably soon lost, Tranter's later models incorporated an attached lever fitted alongside the barrel. Early Adams revolvers had used a bullet cast with a small tail to which a wad was attached. These were designed to fit tightly but could be pushed home with the finger. Adams later adopted a single-lever loading designed by John Rigby in 1854, but in 1855 James Kerr designed a more effective lever and this was the model selected by Tranter.

In 1856 Tranter patented a more conventional, single-trigger revolver. Externally this weapon looked the same as a Beaumont Adams except for a small lug projecting down through the rear of the trigger guard. When this was pressed by the trigger it operated the firing action. Both Tranter's and Adams' revolvers used a solid frame in which barrel, trigger and cylinder housing all formed a complete unit. Tranter paid Adams a royalty, for this had been one of the features of his patent. Like the Adams, Tranter revolvers were imported, particularly by the South, during the American Civil War.

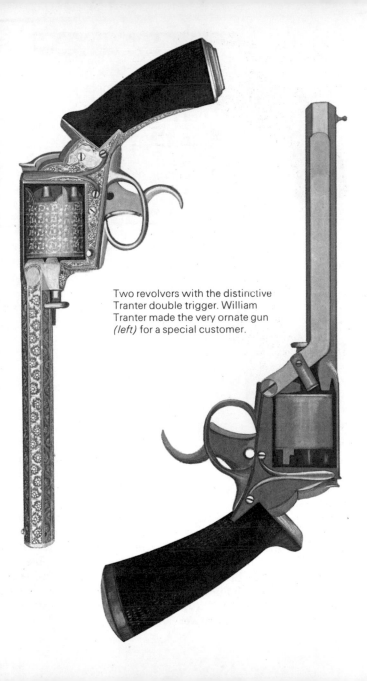

Two revolvers with the distinctive Tranter double trigger. William Tranter made the very ornate gun *(left)* for a special customer.

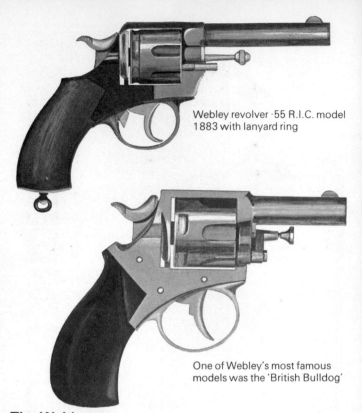

Webley revolver ·55 R.I.C. model
1883 with lanyard ring

One of Webley's most famous
models was the 'British Bulldog'

The Webley

Philip and John Webley of Birmingham were long connected
with the gun trade and by 1833 were producing percussion
revolvers. Their revolvers differed in shape from almost all
other British weapons and were to remain unaltered for a long
period, almost a trademark.

A gracefully down-curving butt had a clean line lacking the
spur so often found on British revolvers. There was a long,
backward projection from the top of the hammer which
earned the name Longspur for the Webley. Many Webley
revolvers, as well as those by other makers, had a small recess
with a spring-closed lid in the base of the butt to hold percussion caps. The Webley loading lever was simple, with a
straight arm parallel to the lower frame of the cylinder housing.

The percussion revolvers made by Webley did not use a solid frame but preferred the Colt style. In this method the barrel was screwed, or locked, on to a central spigot by means of a wedge which engaged with a slot. This style of construction was generally abandoned during the 1860s. Webleys continued to produce revolvers, including pin-fire models and the firm prospered, expanding its activities to produce such things as handcuffs and gunmakers' accessories.

In 1887 the firm received its first order for revolvers to be supplied to the British Government – 10,000 at a cost of six shillings each. The rugged, reliable Webley was to see military service all over the world for many years.

The Army model took a metal centre-fire cartridge and had a frame which broke at the centre allowing easy access to the cylinder for loading. An automatic, spring-operated arm ejected the used cartridge cases.

One very unusual and interesting variant was the Webley–Fosberry automatic revolver first marketed in 1901. In this weapon, after the first manual cocking, expanding gas was used to re-cock the action automatically. It was claimed that twelve shots could be fired in twenty seconds.

The Webley revolver in a First World War trench. It was used by the British Army until well into World War II.

Shoulder stocks

Hand-held firearms are never as accurate as those fired from the shoulder as they suffer from a number of disadvantages. Accuracy is greatly influenced by the length of barrel which in a handgun must obviously be fairly short – seldom more than seven inches although some models like the Colt Buntline did have barrels of twelve inches.

Another important factor in accuracy is steadiness at the moment of firing, for the tiniest degree of shake is greatly multiplied at ranges greater than a few yards. One way in which gunmakers could ensure steadiness was to provide a two-handed grip, but with a pistol this was not easy.

For cavalry purposes, firearms were needed that were accurate at longer ranges than the usual revolvers. A rifle was a little too large to be managed on horseback with comfort, and most cavalry units were equipped with carbines. These were, in effect, short rifles, although the name had originally applied to the calibre rather than the size of weapon.

Even a carbine could be a hindrance, and one compromise solution was the use of a pistol which could be changed to a shoulder weapon by the attachment of a stock. These shoulder stocks were usually made to attach to the butt by means of a metal tongue which engaged with a metal-lined slot cut into the wood. Some form of screw was often used to secure the two items.

Henry Nock, a famous London gunmaker, had supplied double-barrelled pistols with such a butt for the Royal Horse

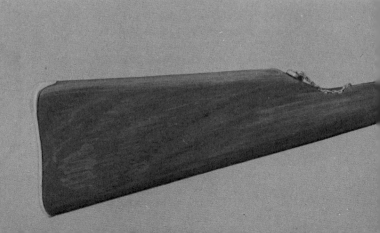

Artillery in 1793, although it was then described as a shifting butt. Some percussion pistols were also made with such butts, but they probably became most popular with the advent of revolvers. Many of Colt's models were made with studs on each side of the metal frame for the attachment of butts, described in his advertisements as carbine breeches.

This type of weapon must not be confused with those produced with a revolving cylinder, which were true longarms. English makers do not appear to have favoured this idea.

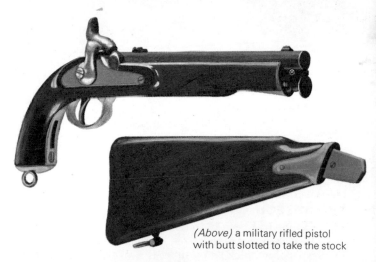

(Above) a military rifled pistol with butt slotted to take the stock

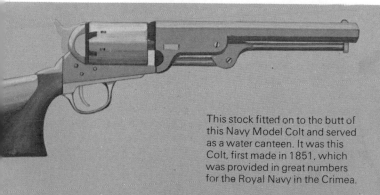

This stock fitted on to the butt of this Navy Model Colt and served as a water canteen. It was this Colt, first made in 1851, which was provided in great numbers for the Royal Navy in the Crimea.

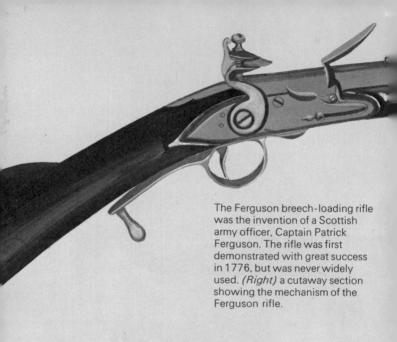

The Ferguson breech-loading rifle was the invention of a Scottish army officer, Captain Patrick Ferguson. The rifle was first demonstrated with great success in 1776, but was never widely used. *(Right)* a cutaway section showing the mechanism of the Ferguson rifle.

THE BREECH-LOADER

Early cannon had been breech-loading with powder and shot inserted at the rear of the barrel, a form of loading which was unquestionably quick and simple. However, it was a difficult principle to apply to small handguns or longarms. Unless there was a very tight join between the unit containing the charge and the barrel, there was a leakage of gases which meant a loss of power and a potential danger to the firer.

There had been many attempts to overcome this problem and though some were successful, all had been either expensive to make or so complex that the production was beyond most gunmakers. Many early attempts had been based on the use of a metal container – in effect a cartridge – holding the powder and placed into a hinged section of the barrel.

In the Tower of London are two such wheel-lock guns which once belonged to Henry VIII. A small trap door at the breech was opened to admit the insertion of the iron cartridge

which, when the trap door was closed, was held firmly in position by a metal block.

An alternative method to the separate cartridge was the screw breech which could be opened rapidly to allow access and then closed tightly for firing. One of the best known, although by no means the earliest, was that designed by Captain Patrick Ferguson of the British Army.

His rifle had a plug cut with an interrupted screw thread and attached to the trigger guard. One turn was sufficient to withdraw the plug, allowing powder and ball to be inserted directly into the breech. If the guard were then turned back the breech was effectively sealed and after priming the pan the weapon was ready to fire.

One hundred such rifles were supplied to the British Army and despite the fact that it proved simple to operate, accurate and reliable, the idea was never exploited. A number of Ferguson rifles were made for the East India Company as well as for private persons.

The needle gun

Early musketeers had relied on their powder flasks or bando-
liers for their supply of powder but the advantages of cartridges were so apparent that they were used quite early on.

Paper had been rolled around a wooden former, one end
tied and the tube filled with powder and the other end closed.
When loading, the soldier tore, or bit, the cartridge and
poured the powder down the barrel, following it with a ball
and then priming the pan. Soon it was common practice to
enclose the lead bullet inside the paper tube although, of
course, priming was still a separate operation. Many attempts
were made to unite priming sequences with the cartridge but
few were really successful. It was the advent of the percussion
system that enabled inventors to produce a reasonable answer.

As early as 1812 a Swiss, Johannes Samuel Pauly patented
what was, in effect, a centre-fire metal cartridge but, as with
other innovations, it was not widely adopted or exploited by
the gun trade. Other inventors produced cartridges which
were consumed in the explosion while others tried to produce
effective metal cartridges. All had some inherent weakness
and it was not until the middle of the nineteenth century
that a really efficient, breech-loading cartridge-using weapon
was produced.

At one time Pauly had working with him a Prussian, Johan
Nikolaus Von Dreyse, who was later to produce the first
effective military breech-loading weapon – the needle gun.
The central feature was a cartridge which was complete in itself,
containing powder, ball and, most important, the igniting
agent. Into the base of the bullet was fitted a small primer of
detonating compound in direct contact with the powder.
When it was struck, the primer immediately ignited the
powder. In order to strike the fulminate the gun had a long,
thin, spring-operated needle which pierced the cartridge
covering, passed through the powder and struck the fulminate.
To insert the cartridge a bolt was withdrawn to allow access
to the breech; this was then closed and locked in position.

The needle gun had two inherent weaknesses. There was a
pronounced escape of gas and flame from the breech and the
long needle was very susceptible to breakage. Despite these
defects the weapon was still a great technical advance.

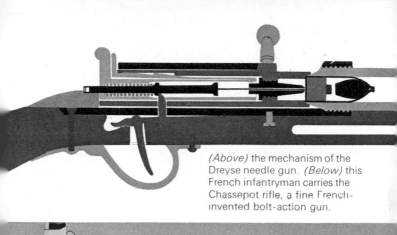

(Above) the mechanism of the Dreyse needle gun. (Below) this French infantryman carries the Chassepot rifle, a fine French-invented bolt-action gun.

Cartridges

In 1829 Clement Pottet patented a cartridge with a separate base which contained a percussion cap. In 1835 Casimir Lefaucheux produced the pin-fire cartridge which had the cap set inside a metal base at the bottom of a short metal rod. A small slot in the chamber of the gun allowed the falling hammer to strike the tip of the rod and detonate the cap. Pin-fire cartridges were very susceptible to damage and it was soon found preferable to deposit the fulminate directly around the inside of the cartridge base where a blow from the hammer was sufficient to detonate the compound. In the rim-fire cartridge, the deposit was limited to the rim only. S. Morse patented in 1856 a cartridge with walls soft enough to expand on the explosion, sealing the chamber. Colonel Edward Boxer developed the idea, for in 1866 he produced a coiled brass

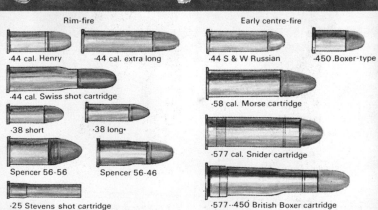

Paper

Combustible

Separa

Rim-fire

·44 cal. Henry

·44 cal. extra long

·44 cal. Swiss shot cartridge

·38 short

·38 long·

Spencer 56-56

Spencer 56-46

·25 Stevens shot cartridge

Early centre-fire

·44 S & W Russian

·450 .Boxer-type

·58 cal. Morse cartridge

·577 cal. Snider cartridge

·577-·450 British Boxer cartridge

cartridge which, in 1885, was replaced by a solid-drawn brass cartridge case. With this step the sequence was complete and the cartridge has remained basically unaltered since the 1880s.

(Below) the cartridges illustrated against the dark background are:
Paper: 1) ·54 calibre, American pistols 1820–1850; 2) ·54 blank;
3) ·64 calibre carbine; 4) ·58 calibre rifle.
Combustible: 1) ·58 calibre skin; 2) ·44 calibre; 3) ·52 calibre linen;
4) paper-covered shot.
Separate-primed: 1) ·54 calibre; 2) ·50 calibre Smith; 3) ·56 calibre
Billinghurst requa
Self-contained: 1) 11 mm. French needle-fire; 2) German rim-type
9·95 mm ; 3) 90 bore needlegun; 4) 16 gauge reloadable steel shell.
Patent ignition: 1) 15 mm. pin-fire; 2) 20 gauge French shotgun;
3) ·58 calibre Gallager and Gladding pin-fire; 4) ·25 calibre copper
case lip-fire; 5) ·30 copper cup-primer; 6) ·50 calibre Crispin.

·rimed   Self-contained   Patent ignition

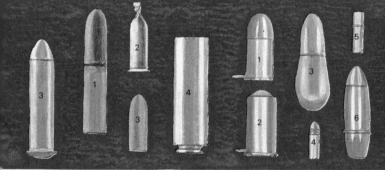

Centre-fire (inside primed)   Modern centre-fire

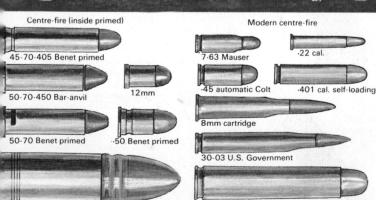

45-70-405 Benet primed

7·63 Mauser

·22 cal.

50-70-450 Bar-anvil

12mm

·45 automatic Colt

·401 cal. self-loading

50-70 Benet primed

·50 Benet primed

8mm cartridge

30-03 U.S. Government

One-inch inside-primed Gatling gun cartridge
with 8 ounce bullet

English Kynoch ·600 nitro cartridge

Smith and Wesson

The modern breech-loading revolver can be said to be the brain child of two American gunmakers, Horace Smith and Daniel Wesson. These two far-sighted men had been responsible for some fine conventional firearms but they were anxious to break into the revolver market.

They experimented with cartridges in which they covered the base with fulminate but found that the detonation caused the base to bulge and so jam the mechanism. They then restricted the priming to the outside edge of the case to produce what is known as a rim-fire cartridge. Ignition was caused by the hammer striking anywhere on the rim.

Smith and Wesson next examined the possibility of having a cylinder into which the cartridge could be inserted from the rear, but they found that this idea had already been patented. In April 1855 Rollin A. White had been granted a patent for cylinders which were bored right through to take the cartridge. Wasting no time the two men approached White, purchased his rights and were soon tooling up ready to go into production with the first cartridge, rear-loading revolvers.

By November 1857 Smith and Wesson were producing the first of a long line of revolvers – a seven-shot, ·22 calibre

Jesse James' Schofield-Smith and Wesson six-shot revolver

Smith & Wesson Model No. 1 used a ·22 rim-fire cartridge 1860–68

Frederic Remington's picture of a street fight shows the antagonists using single-action Colts

revolver. It was an immediate success. For loading, the revolver broke pivoting upwards on the front of the frame over the top of the cylinder.

Holding a virtual monopoly of the field, Smith and Wesson were able to flourish but they were limited by the problems of producing weapons to fire a larger bullet than the small ·22. The case had to be thin enough to allow the blow from the hammer to explode the fulminate and this meant that large charges would split the metal. A new process of hardening copper made it possible to produce cases capable of holding a charge sufficient for a bullet of ·32 calibre. Rollin White's patent expired in April 1869 and a flood of such revolvers with bored-through cylinders followed. In 1870 Smith and Wesson produced a ·44 revolver which was ordered in bulk by the Russian government – 150,000 in seven years.

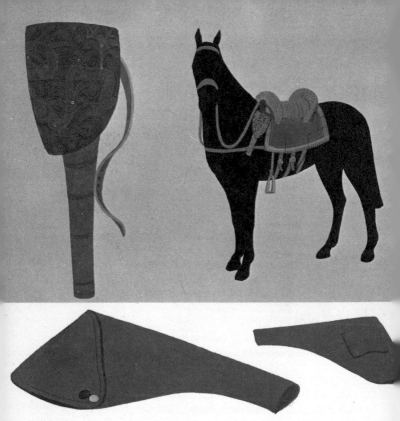

(Top) a 17th-century saddle holster for wheel-lock pistols. *(Bottom)* a belt holster for an Adams revolver.

Saddle and belt holsters

Most early military pistols were, of course, intended for cavalry use and some means of carrying them was essential. The most usual arrangement was to have a pair of leather holsters fitted to the front of the saddle, one hanging on each side of the horse. Many had the rim strengthened with a brass edging and those of the seventeenth and eighteenth centuries were frequently fitted with a large flap to cover the open top and guard against damp and dirt.

Horse holsters continued in use until the early part of the nineteenth century when the pepperbox and revolver

Back and front views of a saddle
holster for a flintlock pistol

removed the necessity of
carrying two pistols.

Smaller, multishot revolvers made it possible for a man
on foot to carry a personal
firearm and belt holsters
made their appearance. Usually of leather, with a fold over
the top, they were secured to
a waist belt by means of loops.
Some open-top holsters had a
strap which crossed over to
hold the revolver in place
and others had a simple loop
which hooked over the
hammer to serve the same
purpose. Despite the persist-
ent legend of the Western
gunman with his holster tied
low down on his thigh, ex-
amination of the many surviving photographs of the
period 1850–90 show that
most holsters were, in fact,
worn fairly high at the waist.

Most military holsters were
designed to be worn on the
right side with the butt projecting forward to be drawn
by the left hand, for it was
assumed that the right hand
would be occupied with
sword or reins. Some automatic pistols, such as the
Mauser, had wooden holsters
so that they could be fitted to
the butt as a shoulder stock.

The sub-machine gun

The adoption of the centre-fire metal cartridge opened up the way for a number of impressive developments in firearms design. From the ordinary five- or six-shot revolver, gun-makers looked forward to producing weapons capable of firing twenty, a hundred or more shots from one loading.

A few revolvers were made with imposing cylinders holding impossibly large numbers of shots but they were never much more than curiosities. During the 1880s there were many experiments aimed at producing a weapon capable of firing a large number of shots in bursts. Soon inventors, such as Maxim, were producing heavy machine guns capable of high rates of fire. However, this type of gun was heavy and bulky and the development of trench warfare during World War I emphasized the need for a light, portable machine gun, firing smaller cartridges but operating on the same principle as the heavier weapons.

This type of gun was to be known as the sub-machine gun. The first steps in its development seem to have taken place in Italy in 1915 when a twin-barrel, anti-aircraft gun, firing a 9 mm Luger pistol cartridge, was used.

The idea was taken up and improved and the Germans produced the MP 18 which had a thirty-two shot, circular magazine fitted on the left-hand side of the gun. Basically, the action was operated by the reaction of the explosion pushing back the moving bolt which held the firing pin. As the bolt moved back it compressed a spring which, in turn, forced the bolt forward again and the backward and forward movement was made to eject the empty case and insert a fresh one into the breech. This reciprocating movement continued for just as long as there was a cartridge to activate the bolt or until the trigger was released.

One of the best known of these sub-machine guns was the Tommy Gun or Thompson machine gun. This was designed by an American, General Thompson. It was first demonstrated in 1920 and was soon in production with a variety of magazine fittings including a monster one holding a hundred rounds. It saw considerable service during World War II. Other makes were developed with an emphasis on smallness and cheapness and many were made with folding butts.

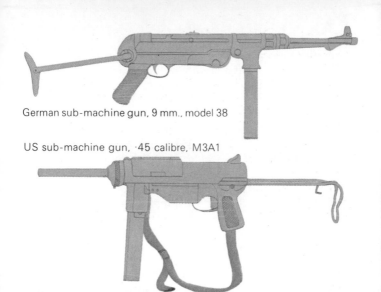

German sub-machine gun, 9 mm., model 38

US sub-machine gun, ·45 calibre, M3A1

(Below) the Thompson ·45 calibre sub-machine gun

The Colt Single-Action Army Model

Smith and Wesson gained a certain limited supremacy in the field of revolver production with the introduction of their metal cartridge but their monopoly ended in April 1869. Naturally other manufacturers had been experimenting in preparation for this date and Colt, Remington and other top firms were ready. There had been many attempts to evade the restrictions set out by the patents held by Smith and Wesson which prevented the use of a cylinder bored through to allow rear loading, but in general they had been unsatisfactory.

In 1873 Colts marketed their most famous revolver – the Single Action Army Model. This model was to stay in production, with one break, right up to the present day. Frontier and Peacemaker were just two of the names this revolver acquired and it was produced in numerous barrel lengths and in a variety of calibres.

It took six cartridges loaded in by means of a gate at the side and the empty cases were hand-ejected by means of a spring-loaded rod mounted beneath the barrel. When all shots had been fired the gate was opened and the cylinder rotated to line up each chamber opposite the rod which was then pushed through to eject the case. As it was a single-action weapon the hammer had to be pulled back, or cocked, before each shot. Some exponents claimed that the 'fanning' of the hammer was a fast method of firing. To do this the trigger was pressed and the hammer cocked with a sweeping action of the flat of the hand; since the trigger was depressed the hammer did not engage in the cocked position but flew forward to fire the cartridge, a movement which could be repeated very rapidly.

A few of these weapons were made with very long barrels, twelve inches and sixteen inches. Later, in 1877, Colts produced a double action revolver, the Lightning, to be followed in 1889 by a fresh departure – the New Navy Double Action, which had a swing-out cylinder. To load, the cylinder was pivoted to swing clear of the frame to permit the insertion of the cartridges. When the cylinder was swung out the empty cases were automatically ejected by a spring-activated arm. Similar designs were produced by other makers and apart from the introduction of the immensely powerful Magnum weapons, revolver design has altered but little since then.

(Above) the solid-frame Colt ·38

(Below) the 0·45 ins. Colt 'Frontier' revolver, first manufactured in 1873, was also known as the 'Single-Action Army' revolver.

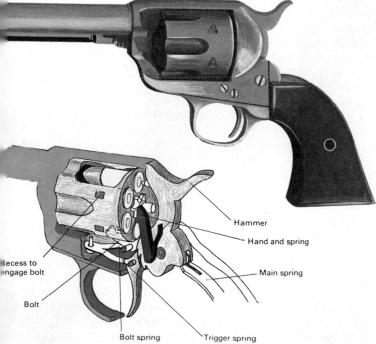

Hammer

Hand and spring

Main spring

Recess to engage bolt

Bolt

Bolt spring

Trigger spring

The mechanism of the Colt 'Frontier' revolver, still being produced today

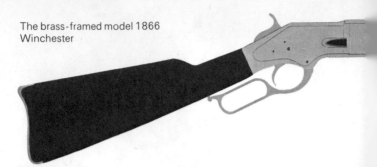

The brass-framed model 1866
Winchester

The 'Gun that won the West'

The 'Gun that won the West' is the somewhat fanciful title given to the lever action, Winchester rifle but it contains sufficient truth to prevent it being ridiculous.

In 1866 the Winchester Repeating Arms Corporation was formed by a shirt manufacturer, Oliver F. Winchester. He had little previous experience in the field of firearms production and viewed it simply as a commercial venture. He had had an interest in the Volcanic Repeating Firearms Company which had produced a repeating pistol with a tubular magazine beneath the barrel. Reloading was achieved by operating a lever connected to the trigger guard. Henry rifles used the same system with a tubular magazine of fifteen rounds and were capable of firing a shot every two and a half seconds, including reloading time. This rifle was made by the New Haven Arms Company which Winchester controlled.

In 1866 a number of changes were made in the Company including the name. A model 1866 Winchester repeating rifle was produced with a brass frame. The shape of this famous weapon was to stay unchanged up to the present day.

Cartridges were loaded into the magazine by way of a spring-loaded gate set at the side of the breech. A coiled spring inside the magazine exerted a pressure so that the last cartridge fed in was pressing against a movable block. As the trigger guard was pulled down the cartridge was withdrawn from the magazine and the hammer cocked. As the lever was lifted the cartridge was fed into the breech and the action locked. After firing, the action was repeated but this time the empty case was also ejected. Firing was rapid and the appearance of the

Henry and Winchester made a tremendous impact on warfare. Indeed there is a story that a Southerner is reputed to have described the Henry as a 'damned Yankee rifle that is loaded on Sunday and fires all week'.

The Winchester played a big role in the opening of the American West

Red Indian guns

Bows, arrows and lances were the original missile weapons of the American Indian and he was skilled in their use, but from the time he first confronted the Colonists he knew how powerful firearms were. Naturally he sought to acquire some of these mighty weapons for his own use.

During the French and Indian Wars both Britain and France supplied arms to those tribes that supported them and on occasions used them against the original suppliers. For the Indian it was necessary to have a sturdy weapon that could be relied on when far from supplies; the flintlock, obtainable from trading posts, was especially valued.

To meet the demand, a number of gunmakers specialized in the production of trade guns. Birmingham gunmakers were prominent in this field and many claimed to be suppliers to the Hudson Bay Company. Indians tended to be rather conservative, demanding an article that they recognized as reliable, and generally preferred a full stocked, flintlock musket firing a ball ·58 inches in diameter. Apparently one particular feature that the Indian demanded was the dragon, or serpentine, side plate which, presumably, had been on the early flintlocks. Later on percussion and cartridge arms were used although US Army reports made after the Battle of the Little Big Horn in 1876 suggest that the number of repeating arms owned by the Indians was small.

Despite the fact that so many Indians fought as light cavalry they do not appear to have favoured handguns, apparently preferring carbines or full-sized muskets. A few handguns of Indian origin have survived but they are rare.

Decoration of longarms and pistols was nearly always simple but colourful, with brass-headed tacks being most popular. Available at trading posts, these were knocked into the butt and stock in simple, geometric patterns and occasionally supplemented by small pieces of mirror and similar baubles set into the stock. Repairs to the stock were often crude but none-the-less effectively carried out by binding it with strips of rawhide or copper wire acquired by cutting the telegraph lines. Captured military weapons, such as Spencers, Winchesters, Henrys and other rifles, were highly prized and bestowed a certain prestige on their owners.

Two paintings by Henry Farny. *(Above)* a Red Indian, carrying a
Winchester rifle, listens to the whine of telegraph wires.

(Below) a captured army scout staked out awaiting torture. The Indian
has a US cavalry issue Spencer repeating rifle.

Eastern guns

When the Portuguese first reached the far islands of Japan they had with them matchlock muskets, the performance of which must have had a profound impact on the Japanese.

The contact with the West was short-lived. The foreigners were soon forbidden the shores of Japan and the country remained closed off until Commander Perry forced contact again in 1854. This isolation meant that the development of firearms in Japan tended to differ from that of Europe and jumped straight from matchlock to cartridge weapons. Flint-lock and percussion Japanese firearms are extremely scarce and there is little documentary evidence to suggest that many were made.

Japanese metalsmiths were among the best in the world and their swords were of superb quality so that it is not surprising that they applied their great skill to the manufacture of barrels of superior quality. Most had very thick walls and were frequently octagonal in section with a thickening at the

European weapons appear in this wood block print of the Japanese Army formed on Western lines by Saigo in the 1870s

muzzle. Silver inlay was often used to decorate the top face of the barrel with simple but pleasing scenes.

Strangely enough, despite their great competence, Japanese metal workers do not seem to have excelled in the production of springs and all seem rather soggy, perhaps because they were fashioned in brass. The type of lock on these Japanese matchlocks was of the design known as snap-lock, a style abandoned in Europe quite early on.

At rest, the arm holding the glowing match was pressed into the priming pan and to make ready for firing the arm was raised, at which point it engaged with a sear, and was held in this position. A small trigger button or lever withdrew the sear allowing the spring to press down the arm. Obviously such a system was very liable to accidental discharge. Stocks of Japanese matchlocks were usually substantial with a very rudimentary butt which was no more than a bulbous end. Inlay of mother of pearl or brass was often used for decoration. A certain number of multibarrel weapons was made too.

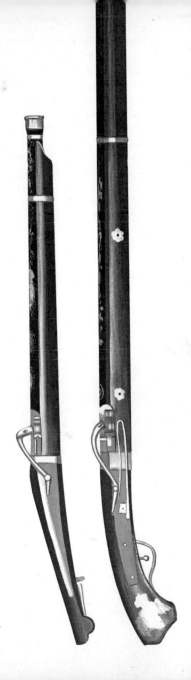

Firearm history and design in India was far more affected by the West than that of Japan, for the contacts were far closer. England and France established a large number of trading stations or factories throughout the country and also raised, trained and equipped their own native armies. As a result, all forms of ignition were used on Indian firearms and local craftsmen copied European weapons as well as adopting imported arms. Matchlock, flintlock and percussion pistols, longarms and blunderbusses were made in a variety of styles and sizes, a tradition of copying which has continued.

Metal workers in Pakistan today still produce hand-made copies of modern rifles and revolvers which are masterpieces of patient skill for every part is hand-made.

Longarms were most common and the majority of these were matchlocks. Asiatic matchlocks almost invariably had the serpentine arranged to swing forward in the direction of the muzzle whereas most European weapons had the arm swinging in the reverse direction. Both matchlocks and flintlocks had rather long barrels, secured to the stock by a series of metal bands or hide thongs. Barrels were often quite elaborate with facets and moulding and occasionally with the muzzle fashioned in the likeness of an animal head. Sights were commonly found on the matchlocks, and trigger guards were usually omitted, although included on most of the flintlocks.

To the north of India, the butt usually had a very pronounced curve whereas the Turks and Persians preferred a much straighter stock with a single sharp step down just behind the breech. Stocks of Turkey and the Caucasus were usually pentagonal in section and often inlaid with mother-of-pearl or other appropriate materials. Tassels and material were commonly used as decoration. One rather uncommon type of firearm produced in Turkey and neighbouring areas was the miniature blunderbuss which was, in effect, a scaled-down version of the normal weapon. They were only about eighteen inches or so long and, presumably, were made for use in one hand and pressed against the thigh when being fired by a man on horseback.

Indian gunmakers in particular seem to have delighted in complex combination weapons and a number of pistol shields and pistol daggers of Indian origin have survived.

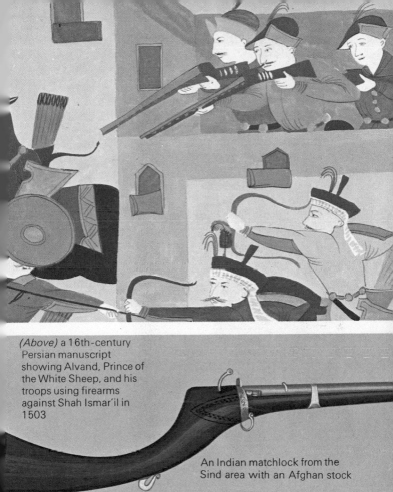

(Above) a 16th-century
Persian manuscript
showing Alvand, Prince of
the White Sheep, and his
troops using firearms
against Shah Ismar'il in
1503

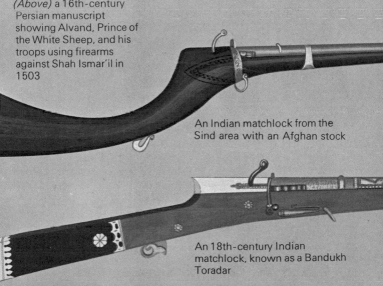

An Indian matchlock from the
Sind area with an Afghan stock

An 18th-century Indian
matchlock, known as a Bandukh
Toradar

Rifles

The principle of rifling or spin had been known from an early date and had been used by archers to improve their accuracy. Broadly speaking, rifling simply cancels out the variations of flight of a projectile by ensuring that the bullet spins about an axis running along the length of the barrel. In order to make the bullet spin, a series of grooves of equal depth are cut on the inside of the barrel and the bullet is made to fit tightly so that its sides are forced into the grooves. As the powder explodes, the gases push the bullet forward and, as it is held so tightly, it follows the grooves which are cut in such a way that they complete one or more full revolutions before the bullet leaves the barrel spinning like a top.

If then the principle was understood why was it not used far more by the earlier gunsmiths? The reason was simply the difficulty of cutting the grooves which was an expensive and tedious job.

Rifled barrels were made from the fifteenth century

The Sharpshooter *(left)* holds a Sharps Infantry rifle, an American breech-loader onwards but cutting the rifling was a slow, laborious business with each spiral groove being done separately. Despite the intricate problems, some very fine barrels were produced by these manual processes and many backwoods gunsmiths made extremely accurate, long-barrelled 'Kentucky' rifles.

As the industrial revolution proceeded, a more capable technology entered into all trades including gunmaking. More reliable machines were soon producing quantities of rifles for the military forces of the world. There was a growth of interest in rifle shooting during the mid-nineteenth century and a great variety of systems were developed with many sizes of grooves and with variations in the number of such grooves.

In Britain, the Enfield rifle became the standard weapon for the British infantry. This rifle fired a ·577'' diameter bullet and had a system of three-groove rifling. A long barrel helped improve its accuracy, and it saw service in many areas of the world.

A ·45–70 trapdoor Springfield and *(far right)* a British Enfield rifle musket

Having accepted that rifles were preferable to smooth bore the British Army had taken one step forward but the remarkable success of the needle gun in the Continental wars made all military authorities think seriously about breech-loading weapons. In Britain it was felt that first of all a stop-gap system, which could convert the large stock of muzzle-loading weapons into breech-loaders, should be adopted.

In 1864 a special committee was set up to examine the problem and make recommendations. Fifty different systems were tested and examined at the great Arsenal at Woolwich and many were immediately rejected, as the leakage of gas or escape of flames from the breeching was far too great for safety. Final choice was the simple but effective system designed by Jacob Snider of New York.

A small section of the breech was removed and a solid block hinged on the right of the barrel was fitted. A plunger passed diagonally through the block emerging at the centre of the face opposite the percussion cap set in the base of the brass cartridge. The usual percussion hammer fitted on the Enfield rifle was retained and as it struck the plunger the blow was transferred, by the plunger, to the cartridge. A spring stud held the breech block closed although on the Mark III model a catch was fitted. Empty cartridge cases were ejected by means of a claw fitted to the front of the breech although the rifle had to be turned over and shaken to remove the cartridge.

Snider-Enfield rifles were satisfactory but obviously a

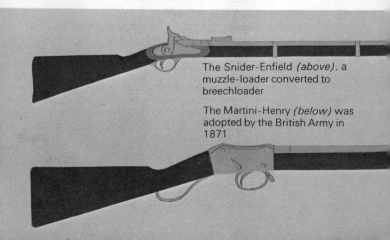

The Snider-Enfield *(above)*, a muzzle-loader converted to breechloader

The Martini-Henry *(below)* was adopted by the British Army in 1871

British troops in battle at Tel-el-Kebir, Egypt, 1882. The British Army in Egypt used both the Snider and the Martini-Henry.

completely new breech-loading weapon was desirable and in October 1867 an Ordnance Committee was set up to select the best model. Two section tests were organized – one to find the most accurate barrel and the other to select a breech-loading mechanism for the new weapon.

A barrel of small calibre ·45″ designed by an Edinburgh gunsmith, Alexander Henry, was selected and adopted in 1871. For the breech action they chose a lever-operated system designed by an Austrian, Friedrich von Martini, patented in 1868. To open the breech the trigger guard was depressed and the cartridge was then inserted. As the lever was raised the

(Above) a Lee experimental rifle and magazine, made at Enfield in 1886. The cutaway drawing *(below)* shows the mechanism of the Lee-Metford Mark II of 1892.

breech block was closed ready for firing. Extraction was automatic. Martini-Henry rifles remained in service until 1891.

Most armies of the world were using breech-loading rifles by the late nineteenth century but the majority were still single-shot and the next step had to be the adoption of a magazine rifle which could be loaded once and fire several shots. Commercial magazine rifles had been in use for some years before the military adopted them. This had been due to a certain amount of reactionary thinking but also to a cautious approach fearing trouble if too hasty a selection were made.

In Britain the Martini-Henry extraction was giving some trouble and in 1883 another committee examined the weapon and recommended certain changes. It was not until 1887 that this committee reported on the problem of selecting a good magazine rifle. Their choice was a box-magazine and a turning bolt action designed by James Lee.

In December 1888 the Lee-Metford magazine rifle was officially adopted by the British Army. The magazine held

five rounds of ·303″ ammunition but with the introduction of more powerful propellants it was found that the barrel suffered from excessive wear and corrosion. Experiments suggested that the problem would be overcome by the use of deeper grooves in the rifling and the Royal Small Arms Factory at Enfield devised a new form of rifling.

In 1895 the Lee-Enfield rifle was introduced and was to remain the standard arm until 1902 when a shorter version was approved. This, the Short Magazine Lee-Enfield, was to continue in service with minor modifications through two world wars and numerous campaigns until replaced by the modern automatic rifle. The magazine could hold ten rounds and could be kept recharged. Constant practice was responsible for the rapid fire for which the British soldier became famous. Such modifications as were made were mainly concerned with sighting and finer details, for the entire weapon showed itself to be perfectly reliable under all conditions.

(Above) said to be the first gas-operated automatic ever made, this weapon was the work of a Spanish gunmaker, Orbea.

(Below, top) the German Luger 9 mm. pistol, a model made in 1908. *(Bottom)* a 1900 model of the Browning 7·65 mm. automatic pistol.

Automatic revolvers

Revolvers were produced in quantity from the 1840s on and became more and more a personal defence weapon. They all required to be recocked before each shot. Cocking might be done by the thumb as in the Colt, or by the trigger finger as in the Adams. Many designers sought to make this action automatic so that the only movement required was the pressing of the trigger to fire each shot.

Although these weapons are usually referred to as automatics the majority of them should, in fact, be more accurately described as self-loading weapons, for a true automatic continues firing as long as the trigger is held down. As the explosion of the propellant exerts an all-round force, this can be used to activate a mechanism which can extract the empty case of the preceding shot and insert a fresh cartridge in the breech. Another system uses the excess gas produced in the explosion to operate the loading mechanism.

Although a few designs had been made earlier, the first weapon produced in any quantity was that designed by Hugo Borchardt and made in Berlin in 1893. A clip of eight cartridges was inserted into the butt and ejection and reloading were achieved by the action of two toggle-like arms fitted at the rear of the barrel and activated by the recoil. This toggle system was simplified and improved by George Luger and in 1898 the first of his famous automatic pistols was produced. Lugers were produced in a variety of models with barrels of differing lengths; some had shoulder stocks. As it was such a reliable weapon many countries adopted it as an official weapon, among them Iran, China and Turkey. In 1896 Peter Mauser produced a ten-shot automatic pistol with the magazine set in front of the trigger guard. Browning, the American firearms manufacturer, produced his first automatic in 1897 and Colt were later to enter the field.

Machine guns

James Puckle had produced a practical machine gun as early as 1718 and there had been other attempts after this. Some had been nothing more than lines of barrels each loaded and then fired by means of a trail of powder. These were known as organ guns. Volley guns with seven barrels had been manufactured by Nock and others but all suffered from the disadvantage that firing was uncontrolled: once the sequence started it continued until the weapon was empty.

A planter living in North Carolina, USA, Richard Gatling, had an inventive turn of mind and during the American Civil War turned his attention to guns. In November 1862 he patented a quick-firing gun which was not a very satisfactory weapon. Three years later Gatling obtained another patent and, as a result of many improvements, the Gatling gun was the first really effective machine gun. In 1866 the United States Army officially adopted the gun and one hundred were ordered. It was basically a system using six revolving barrels, each with a separate bolt, cocking and firing mechanism. Cartridges were fed into a hopper so that gravity caused them

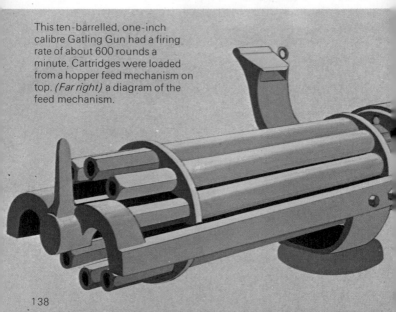

This ten-barrelled, one-inch calibre Gatling Gun had a firing rate of about 600 rounds a minute. Cartridges were loaded from a hopper feed mechanism on top. *(Far right)* a diagram of the feed mechanism.

to drop down into chambers which were then placed in turn into the barrels where a series of cams caused the strikers to move back and then fly forward to fire the cartridge. The whole sequence of events was activated by turning a large crank. This caused the barrels to rotate and move the strikers. The gun maintained a rate of fire of about 300 per minute.

Mounted on a simple carriage, the Gatling was a significant addition to any army's fire power and the British ordered some in 1870 for trials. It was found that the Gatling expended 492 pounds of ammunition to score 2803 hits whilst a 12-pounder field gun used 1,232 pounds of ammunition to obtain 2286 hits. Gatlings saw service in many campaigns including the Zulu War. General Custer refused three of them just before his defeat at the Battle of the Little Big Horn in 1876.

Gas and electricity systems raised the rate of fire to the incredible figure of 3,000 a minute, but newer and less complex systems were being developed and the Gatling was discarded by most nations during the early part of this century. A modern version, the Vulcan, carried by aircraft, achieved a rate of fire of 6,000 rounds a minute.

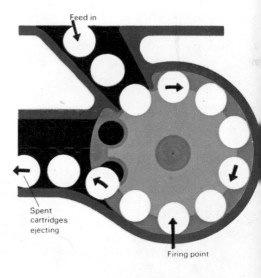

Feed in

Spent cartridges ejecting

Firing point

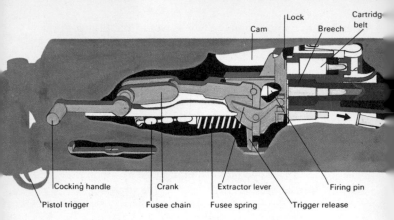

Cam   Lock   Breech   Cartridge belt

Cocking handle   Crank   Extractor lever   Firing pin

Pistol trigger   Fusee chain   Fusee spring   Trigger release

(Above) the mechanism of the Lewis-Maxim machine gun, which was mounted in the nose of World War I DH 2 fighters *(below)*.

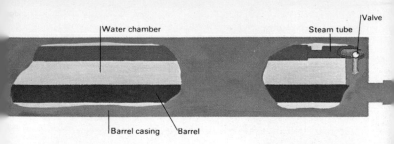

Water chamber · Valve · Steam tube · Barrel casing · Barrel

Gatling relied on the movement of barrels to achieve a high rate of fire and the weapon was essentially a series of six guns each being loaded, fired and emptied in turn. A simpler system would be one which used only one barrel and mechanism which loaded and fired. An American who became a naturalized Britain was the one to supply the answer. Hiram Maxim was of French descent, born in Maine. On a visit to Europe he had his attention drawn to the search for a really good machine gun. He set up a workshop in London and began work. In two years, 1883–5, he patented a number of very sound systems of automatic firing. His first patent was a winner and performed the whole sequence of feeding in cartridges, firing, extracting and ejecting the case completely automatically.

Maxim's gun worked on the recoil principle with the barrel moving only a short distance but with the breech flying back further to extract and eject the case as well as feeding in another round and firing it. It was adopted by the British Army in 1891 and the German Army in 1899. A large bore version, 1·457 inches, known as the pom pom gun was used by both Boers and British in South Africa.

World War I, 1914–18, saw the machine gun adopted more and more and tactics evolved to make use of its terrific fire power. Quick movement made it necessary to produce light weapons as well as the heavier models used in fixed positions.

One of the most versatile of the lighter weapons was the Lewis gun designed by another American, Isaac Lewis, in 1911. It had a rate of 500-600 shots a minute and had a circular magazine fitted above the barrel. Its lightness made it very suitable for aircraft use and it was first fired from an aircraft in 1912. In action it was used by a British plane in 1914.

Sporting guns

Shooting for pleasure has been popular since the earliest days of guns but it was during the eighteenth century that it became most popular. Special guns known as fowling pieces were designed and a great deal of time and trouble was expended in the production of barrels to shoot true. Discussion as to the best type of shot was often heated and most of the great marksmen had their own ideas as to the best combination of powder, wadding and shot.

The small lead balls, known as shot, were manufactured by dropping molten lead into water from the top of a tall tower. Pure lead was too soft and a slight amount of arsenic or other metals was added to it. Size of shot was controlled by pouring the molten lead through a sieve and could be varied from a dust-like shot to pieces ·175 inches in diameter. Cartridges of card with a metal base containing the primer were produced early in the nineteenth century. In 1835 Lefaucheux was granted a patent for a shotgun in which the barrels hinged down to allow the pinfire cartridges to be inserted directly into the breech. Extraction was difficult and there were frequent failures, but the idea was basically sound.

Many kinds of breech-loading systems were designed. Some had the barrels swinging down for loading, others had the barrels moving forward while some had them pivoting sideways. The next step forward was the adoption of the hammerless gun. Again, that is not really an accurate description for there was a hammer, but it was so designed as to be mounted internally. Flintlock weapons had been made with internal mechanism and so had percussion weapons, but the centre-fire cartridge was much better adapted for this style of firing.

As there was no external spur the mechanism could not be cocked manually, and this action had to be performed automatically either with the movement of a lever or that of the closing of the barrels. Automatic ejection was the next feature and it appeared in 1874 in a double-barrelled gun by J. Needham.

Recently the magazine shotgun has become more common. Many versions are available, most of them operated by a pump action. Much effort has been devoted to improving the range and accuracy of shotguns by the choking of barrels. Here the last section of the barrel is made with a smaller bore than the rest, which has the effect of concentrating the shot and increasing the shotgun's range.

Detail of the stock of a Holland and Holland 'Badminton' model double-barrelled shotgun

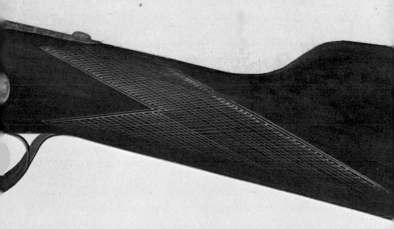

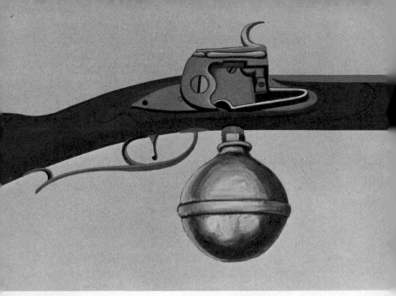

A German air rifle, made about 1800, with a bar lock and brass ball reservoir mounted beneath the barrel

Airguns

Since a bullet is propelled by gas generated by an explosion it is obvious that air pressure can also be used for the same purpose. Airguns are of two types – those that use air compressed in a reservoir and used as required and those in which air pressure is created just before it is used. Those early examples of airguns still surviving are of the second type: pressing the trigger operates a piston and bellows to produce a violent puff of air. As might be expected, the pressure was small and the size of the projectile limited.

During the first half of the seventeenth century a number of airguns with a double-walled barrel was manufactured. In these, the space between the inner and outer barrel served as the reservoir and a head of pressure was built up by the use of a hand pump. Trigger pressure, in one way or another, opened a valve and allowed a burst of compressed air to enter the centre barrel and expel the bullet.

In the eighteenth century the barrel system was replaced by a ball-like reservoir mounted beneath the barrel but this made the gun unsuitable for rough outdoor usage. The butt reservoir was more popular with hunter and poacher alike.

Around 1750 the airgun was often fitted with a detachable butt reservoir which made it possible to carry a number of spares and so leave the pump behind. Many of the airguns of this period were fitted with a lock that had the appearance of a conventional flintlock. The cock opened the valve to allow a burst of air to escape. Since the entire firing mechanism was simple it was not difficult to produce magazine, repeating airguns and one designed by an Italian, Girardoni, was adopted by the Austrian army in 1780. It fired a ·5 in. ball. Naturally the effective range decreased with the number of shots fired making it very difficult for the soldier to take effective aim unless he knew exactly how many shots had been fired.

(Top) late 18th-century air pistol with butt reservoir. *(Centre)* of the same date, this is a German example of a bellows pistol. *(Bottom)* modern American pneumatic ·22 calibre pistol.

Some strange guns

From the time of its introduction gunpowder stimulated designers to produce a range of very strange and devious weapons. Most were planned to serve a double or even treble purpose, and the results were sometimes rather extreme.

One imaginative inventor designed a breastplate fitted with nineteen pistols so the wearer became a one-man barrage. All these rather unusual types are usually grouped together under the title curiosa. Knuckle duster guns were popular during the later part of the nineteenth century and probably the best known is the 'My Friend' which was essentially a pepperbox pistol with a butt pierced to take the little finger. As a first defence it was held in the clenched hand with the butt section projecting below the little finger. A hammer was cocked manually and the trigger was set just in front of the ring section. Some were made with a seven shot ·22″ cylinder, some had five shot ·32 ″ and, more rarely, five shot ·41″.

Tradition has it that somebody suggested to James Reed of New York, the inventor, that it would prove useful when striking someone if the weapon had a barrel fitted, and a number of such weapons were made. To provide several shots many designers used the super-imposed load principle where two charges were loaded, one on top of the other. The front charge was fired first but if a mistake were made the result was usually fatal.

In 1856 Jean Le Mat, a Louisiana doctor, was granted a patent for a double-barrelled revolver designed to fire nine ·42 bullets, using the conventional barrel, and one grapeshot charge

Patented in 1865, this knuckle-duster revolver was named 'My Friend'!

146

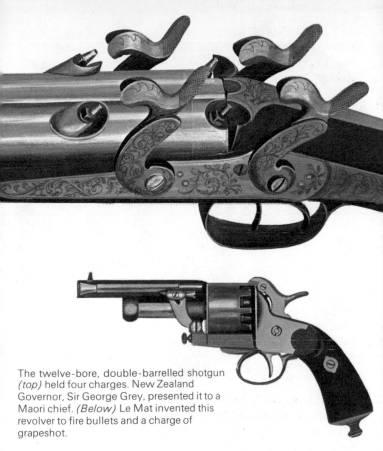

The twelve-bore, double-barrelled shotgun *(top)* held four charges. New Zealand Governor, Sir George Grey, presented it to a Maori chief. *(Below)* Le Mat invented this revolver to fire bullets and a charge of grapeshot.

through the lower barrel. Selection of the barrel to be discharged was made by means of a movable nose fitted on the hammer.

These weapons were used by the Confederates in the American Civil War but were mostly made in France and England. They were made with the percussion cap ignition as well as with pinfire and centre-fire cartridges.

Pistol swords were made in the seventeenth and eighteenth centuries but few pistol knives were ever produced. In this respect the Elgin cutlass pistol is unique. It was patented in July 1837 and was described by its inventor, George Elgin, as

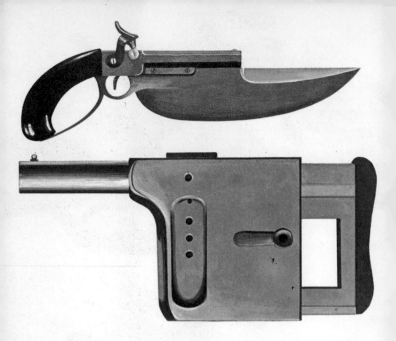

Four very strange weapons. *(Above, top)* an Elgin cutlass pistol; *(bottom)* a Gaulois squeezer pistol. *(Opposite, top)* a French 'Apache' six-shot revolver, with a built-in dagger and knuckle-duster butt; *(bottom)* a palm pistol or squeezer called 'The Protector'.

a Pistol Cutlass or Pistol Knife. One hundred and fifty of these strange weapons were ordered by the US Navy for the use of an expedition setting out to explore the South Seas. Barrels were five inches long whilst the blade was eleven inches in length, but beyond these two features almost every surviving Elgin pistol differs slightly from another – some have hand guards extending between trigger guard and butt but most have not.

In contrast with the heavy appearance of the Elgin pistol the so-called squeezer pistols were small and almost delicate in appearance. Squeezers such as the Gaulois were simple weapons intended to be concealed in the hand and fired by clenching the fist and pressing home the sliding section.

Basically similar to the Gaulois pistol was the Protector revolver which was also held concealed in the hand and then

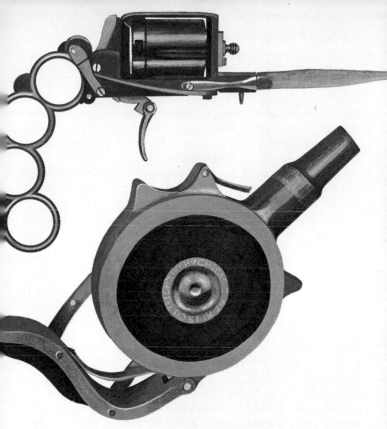

squeezed. This style was patented in 1888 and most examples fired seven ·32 inch cartridges, housed in a round body.

Far more versatile and fearsome was the Dolne or Apache pistol, which was a three-fold weapon — pistol, knife and knuckle duster. The blade was pivoted below the cylinder, as was the trigger. Most were six shot and fired a 7mm pinfire cartridge. Another version made by Delhaxie differed in the arrangement of the component parts but was basically the same. Such weapons were supposed to have been popular with the Paris criminals known as the Apaches.

Knife pistols using both percussion caps and cartridges were produced by the firm of Unwin and Rodgers. These had the appearance of a conventional penknife.

GUN MANUFACTURE

Like that of swords or armour, the early production of firearms tended to be based on certain towns or districts. In Germany Nuremberg held the ascendency in the beginning whilst in France and England the capital cities attracted gunmakers. As the demands of war increased more centres became involved. In Britain there was a gradual decrease in the London gun trade and a corresponding expansion of that in Birmingham. In France arsenals were set up at Charleville and St Etienne, while the American War of Independence encouraged the colonists to found their own arsenals at Harpers Ferry in Virginia and at Springfield, Massachusetts.

At first the production of all firearms was entirely in the hands of craftsmen who made every piece by hand and then assembled the complete weapon. From the late seventeenth century there was a conversion to machine production, slow at first but accelerating in the eighteenth century. Complete conversion came in the nineteenth century. Samuel Colt was probably the first maker to appreciate the enormous potential of machinery in the gun trade. Barrels for shotguns are virtually the only item still largely hand made today, apart from decoration to personal specification.

In the eighteenth century most of the British guns were produced in Birmingham and the parts sent to London for finishing and assembling although clients prepared to pay the price could still have the entire thing made up by the London maker. Each weapon required the services of a number of craftsmen ranging from a lock filer to a 'screwer up'. Thus no two guns or pistols were ever exactly the same.

Barrels were of vital importance, for upon them depended the accuracy of the shot and the life of the shooter, as a weakness could lead to a burst with fatal results. The proving of barrels for weak spots had been carried out in the earliest days but by the seventeenth century it had become a standard practice. Each barrel was loaded with a greater than normal charge of powder which was then fired, and the barrel examined for any cracks or tiny holes. If it was found to be undamaged the barrel was stamped with a recognized mark by the appropriate authority. In Britain, proving was carried out in London and Birmingham. The USA had no set system.

Makers' marks

Amsterdam

Antwerp

Birmingham
Gunmakers' proof mark
After 1813

Denmark & Norway
Reign of Christian IV

Denmark & Norway
Reign of Christian V

Eibar

Essen

Konigsberg

Leyden

Liège

Vienna

London Gunmakers'
Company – View mark

London Gunmakers'
Company – Proof mark

London
'Foreigners' mark'

Maestricht

Nuremberg

Paris

St Etienne

Suhl

Suhl

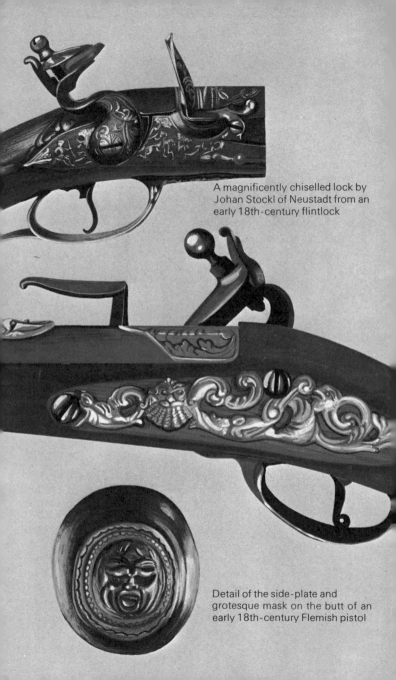

A magnificently chiselled lock by Johan Stockl of Neustadt from an early 18th-century flintlock

Detail of the side-plate and grotesque mask on the butt of an early 18th-century Flemish pistol

DECORATION

Decoration on guns appeared in one form or another at an early date. One of the oldest firearms in existence is fashioned with a head on the barrel. In the Orient this practice was prevalent and continues up to the present, with cannon cast in a variety of fantastic shapes of dragons and monsters.

Inlay was an early style of decoration with the stock cut to accommodate small plaques or shapes of mother-of-pearl, horn, ivory, gold, silver, steel and precious stones. In Europe some of the most gorgeously decorated weapons were wheel-locks with inlay, chiselled steel mounts and gold and silver decoration on stock and barrel. With the adoption of the snaphaunce and flintlock stock, decoration on British weapons tended to be restricted to simple carving around the barrel tang and lock.

On the Continent there was a more flamboyant approach. Many of the high class sporting guns had the stocks, particularly around the butt, carved with animals heads or delicate tracery. In Brescia and other parts of central and northern Italy the chiselling of steel became a speciality. Barrels were often so decorated, and wheels, locks, trigger guards and butt caps were carved with figures or intricate tracery. In Belgium at the Liège arms centre it was common to chisel small ovals with portraits in them. Steel inlay was also a speciality with steel cut so delicately as to resemble lace and then set neatly and carefully into corresponding channels cut into the wood. In Britain metal inlay was rather simpler and the most common style was that of silver wire inlay.

Barrels were often browned. This was done by treating the surface of the metal with any one of a dozen formulae. Rusting took place and then was scraped off and the process repeated several times until the required colour was achieved, when the barrel was washed and gently polished. Not only was the effect attractive but it also served to resist the ravages of rust.

Later, barrels and other metal parts were blued by a heating and cooling process. Again, the skin formed was protective as well as pretty. On the more expensive items there might well be some gold inlaid letters or words. On pistols of the Balkans and Near East the style of decoration was far more florid than that of West Europe and silver wire, silver plates, coral, precious stones and materials were all pressed into service.

MODERN GUNS

There has been a general tendency amongst military planners today to arm their infantry with self-loading or automatic rifles in place of the earlier magazine weapons. There has also been a general move towards standardization of ammunition and the use of a smaller calibre bullet – much of the world now uses 7·62mm ammunition.

Newer and powerful propellants have ensured that the bullets are now much more powerful with much higher muzzle velocities. The early Tommy Gun had a muzzle velocity of 920 feet per second, compared with the present Russian AK47 Assault Rifles 2329 fps and the 2800 fps of the US M.14 rifle.

Newly developed materials and techniques have been pressed into service to produce light, but very rugged weapons. The Armalite AR10 uses steel for the barrel and bolt and little else, with chromium plating to resist rusting; total weight is $7\frac{1}{2}$ lbs compared with the Thompson at 11 lbs.

In the area of competition and target shooting increasingly complex stocks have appeared with all manner of weights and projections designed to facilitate aiming. Many shotguns are now made with magazines so that they can fire several times without reloading. Airguns are now often powered by small cylinders of compressed carbon dioxide.

Experiments are going on into the possibilities of weapons using rocket powered missiles and at least one such pistol has been marketed. Ironically, alongside all these advances there has been a tremendous increase of interest in the collecting, shooting and study of antique firearms. In many countries – Italy, Japan and Belgium – factories manufacture replicas of such famous weapons as the Kentucky rifle, Colt percussion revolvers and many of the early rifles. Many shooters, in search of consistent and accurate shooting, now reload their own cartridges so that in many ways the wheel has turned full circle through the phase of craftsmen hand-making each piece of a gun, through increasing mechanization and the production of standard ammunition back to the beginning with more people interested in hand-made individual weapons.

The American self-loading Armalite AR 10 rifle used in Vietnam represents the most modern trends in firearms

BOOKS TO READ

Among the many books which have been published on the history and manufacture of firearms, the following are generally available from publishers or bookshops, or through public libraries.

The Age of Firearms by Robert Held. Cassell, London, 1957.

The Book of the Gun by Harold L. Peterson. Paul Hamlyn, London, 1963.

Encyclopedia of Firearms edited by Harold L. Peterson. Connoisseur, London, 1968.

Firearms by Howard L. Blackmore. Studio Vista, London, 1964.

Firearms by Howard Ricketts. Weidenfeld & Nicolson, London, 1962.

Firearms Collecting for Amateurs by James Henderson. Frederick Muller, London, 1966.

Guns by Warren Moore. Grosset & Dunlap, New York, 1963.

Guns by Dudley Pope. Weidenfeld & Nicolson, London, 1965; Spring Books, London, 1969.

Guns and Rifles of the World by Howard L. Blackmore. Batsford, London, 1965.

One Hundred Great Guns by Merrill Lindsay. Blandford Press, London, 1968.

Small Arms by Frederick Wilkinson. Ward Lock, London, 1965.

Swords and Daggers by Frederick Wilkinson. Ward Lock, London, 1967.

Warrior to Soldier 449–1660 by A. V. B. Norman and Don Pottinger. Weidenfeld & Nicolson, London, 1966.

INDEX

Page numbers in bold type refer to illustrations.

Adams, Robert 100, **100**, 102
Airgun 144–145, 154
AK47 154
America 63–64
American Indian guns 124, **125**
Amsterdam 60
Arabs 8
Armalite AR10 154
Arquebus 17, **23**
Arrow 6, 10, **19**
Artillery 4–7

Bacon, Roger 8, **8**
Ball trigger 57, **57**
Ballista 5, **5**
Baltic Lock 6
Bandolier 26
Barrel, cannon 12–13
  turn off 50, 54, **54**
Barrel key 54
Bayonet 72, **81**
  plug 72
  socket 73
  spring 72, **72, 73**
Bayonne 72
Beaumont, F. 101, 102
Belling 70
Belt hook 57, **57**, 62
Berthold, Black 9, **9**
Birmingham 64, 101, 102, 104, 124, 150
Blueing 60, 153
Blunderbuss 70–71, **72**, 73, 84, 128
Bolt 110, 118
Bolt (crossbow) 7
Borchardt, Hugo 137
Boutet, Nicolas 60
Bow **19**
Boxer, Edward 112
Boxlock 54, 69, 84
Breech-loader 108–149
Brescia 46, 60, 153
Brown Bess 64, **64**, 65
Browning 137
Bullet 102
Bullet mould 95, **95**

Caliver 22
Cannon 10–15, **19**
  breech-loading **12, 13**

Cannon-ball 11, **11**
Cannoneer **17**
Carbine 34, **53**, 65, 106
Cartridge 74, 80, **91**, 105, 108, 110, 112–113, **112–113**, 122, 132, 147
  paper 65, **112**
  pin-fire 112, 142
  rim-fire 112, 114
Cartridge pouch **81**
Catapult 5, **5**
Charleville 150
China 8
Choking 143
Cock 45, 46, 49, 53, 58, 69, **92**, 101
Collier, Elisha 96, **96**
Colt, Samuel 98, **98**, 100, 150
Colt, Buntline 106
  Dragoon 99
  Frontier 120, **121**
  Lightning 120
  Navy 99, 100, **107**
  New Navy 120
  Peacemaker 120
  Single Action Army 120
Combier, Jehan 15
Combination weapons 34–35, **34–35, 43, 75**, 146–149, **146, 148, 149**
Crossbow 7, **7**, 18, 34
Cutter **95**
Cylinder 99, 101, 107, 118, 120

Da Vinci, Leonardo **28**, 29
Dafte, John **53**
Dardanelles Gun 15, **15**
Decoration 153
Devillers, H. **69**
Dog lock 53
Dogshead 30
Doune 57
Duel **36–37**

Egg, Durs 78, **91**
Ejector 105, 122, 132, 143
Elgin, George 147, **148**
Envoy, Joseph **97**

Ferguson, Patrick 109
Firing pin 118
Flint 45
Flintlock 34, 48–87, 128

continental 60, **61**
Florence 10
Forsyth, Alexander **88**, 89, 90
Fowling piece **53, 78, 88**, 142
Freeman, James **54**
French lock 49
Frizzen 49, 54, 58, 69, 84, 92, 94
Frobisher, Martin **40**
Full cock 99
Fulminate 89, 90, 91, 92

Gatling, Richard 86, 138
Girardoni 145
Glockenthon, Nicholaus **20**
Gum arabic 90
Gun, knuckle duster 146, **146**, 149, **149**
  manufacture 150–152
  organ 138
  percussion 89–107
  Puckle 86, **87**
  sporting 78, **78, 79**, 93, 142–143
  volley 84, 138
Gunpowder 8–9, 82
Guthrie 90

Hair trigger 43
Hakenbüchse 17
Halberd **29**
Half cock 52, 69
Hammer 94, 99, 101, 112, 120, 132
Hammerless action 143
Hand-cannon **16**
Handgun 16–19, 84
Hangfire 89
Harman, John **68**
Harper's Ferry 63, 150
Hartford 98
Henry, Alexander 133
Holster 68, 95
  belt **116**, 117
  saddle 116–117, **116, 117**
Hunting 78

India 128
Indian guns 128, **129**

Japan 126–127
Javelin 5

Kerr, James 102
Knubley and Browne **68**

Landsknecht 21
Le Bourgeoys, Marin 49
Le Mat, Jean 146, **147**
Le Page 41
Lee, James 134
Lefaucheux, Casimir 112,
142
Lewis, Isaac 141
Liège 60, 153
Loading lever 101, 102, 104
London 64, 98, 101, 150
Longarms 53
seventeenth-century
52-53
Long-bow 6, **6**, 18
Longspur 104
Luger, George 137

M3 A1 **119**
M14 154
Mace **34**
Machine-gun 118, 138–141
Gatling 138–139,
138–139
Lewis 141
Lewis-Maxim **140**
Maxim 141
Puckle 86, **87**
Madrid lock 59
Magazine **87**, **89**, 122, 134,
135, 143, 145
Magnum 120
Manton, Joseph 78, **78**, 90
Martini, Friedrich von 133
Match 21, 22
Matchlock **20**, 21–27, 35,
84, 126, 128, **129**
Mauser, Peter 137
Maxim, Hiram 118, 141
Maximilian I **20**
Micro-rifling 97
Milemete, Walter de 10, **10**
Military weapons 62–66
Miquelet lock 58, **58**
Missile weapons 6–7
Modern weapons 154–155
Monk's Gun **28**, 29
Mons Meg 14, **14**
Morse, Samuel 112
Mortar, hand **17**
MP18 118
Multi-barrel weapons
38–39, 84, **84**, **85**
Multi-shot weapons 84
Musket **21**, 22, **23**, 52, 64,
64
Musket drill 24–25, **24–25**

Musketeer **21**, 72

Navy Colt 99, 100, **107**
Needham, J. 143
Needle gun 110, **111**, 132
Nipple 92, 99
Nipple key **95**
Nock, Henry 65, **68**, 78
106, 138
North, Simeon 63
Nuremberg 150

Orbea **136**

Pan 22
waterproof 78
Parkhouse **95**
Patch box 77
Paterson Colt 98
Pauly, Johannes Samuel
110
Pech, Peter **39**
Pepperbox 94, **94**, **95**, 97,
116
Percussion cap **90**, 91, **91**,
92, 93, 94, **94**, 99, 104,
112
Percussion lock **89**, 90
Perry, Commander 126
Persia **129**
Pike 72
Pikeman 72
Pistoia 37
Pistol 73, **73**, 74, 84, **84**, **85**
air 145, **145**
Apache **148**, 149
automatic **136**, 137
Browning 137
duck's foot 84
duelling 66, **67**
eighteenth-century 54–55
flintlock **48**
Gaulois 148, **148**
Highland *see* Scottish
Luger 118, 137
military 62, 63
Miquelet 58–59, **59**
muff 68
percussion **92**, 128
pocket 68, **68**, 69, 85, **90**,
93, 99
Queen Anne 54–55
repeating 122
rifled **107**
Ripoll 59
snaphaunce **47**
Scottish 56–57, **57**
Spanish 58–59, **59**
squeezer 148

top-action 84, **85**
top-hammer **90**
turn-over **85**
wheel-lock 36–39,
36–39
Pistol knife 75, 147, 149
Pistol sword 74, **74**, **75**, 147
Pom pom 141
Pottet, Clement 112
Powder flask **26**, **27**, 32–33
32–33, 66, 80, **80**, 81, 95
Powder horn 27, 33, **80**, 81,
81
Powder tester **82**, 83, **83**
Pricker 57, **81**
Primer 110
Priming 22
pan 69, 84
Proofing 60, 150
Puckle, James 86, 96, 138
Pyrites 29, 30

Ramrod 22, 54, 62, 64, 69,
75, 95
Ramshorn butt 57, **57**
Reed, James 146
Remington, Frederic **115**
Rest 22
Revolver **46**, 53, 94, 96, **97**,
98, **99**, 116, 118, **147**
Adams 100–101, **101**,
102, **116**
automatic 105, 137
British Bulldog **104**
Colt **115** ((*see also* Colt)
double-action 120
double-trigger 102, **103**
flintlock **96**
percussion 105
pin-fire 105
Protector 148, **148**
Schofield **114**
self-cocking 101
self-loading 137
single-action 120
Smith and Wesson
114–115
transition 95, 97
Tranter 102, **103**
Webley 104, **104**, 105,
105
Rifle 76–77, 130–136
air 144, **144**
Chassepot **111**
Enfield 131, **131**, 135
Ferguson **108**, 109, **109**
Henry 122, 124
Jaeger 77
Kentucky **76**, 77, 131
Lee **134**
Lee-Enfield 135

Lee-Metford 134, **134**, **135**
lever-action 122
Martini-Henry **132**, 134
Pennsylvania 76, **76**
percussion **93**
Sharps **130**
Short Magazine Lee-Enfield 135
Snider 132
Snider-Enfield 132, **132**
Spencer 124, **125**
Springfield **131**
wheel-lock 42–43, **43**
Winchester 122, **122**, **123** 124, **125**
Rigby, John 102
Rocket 8
Roman Candle Gun 39, **39**, 70, 97

Safety catch 69
St Etienne 150
Scent-bottle **00**, 00, **00**, 00
Sciopetto **18**
Sear 30, 45, 46, 49, 52
Self-priming 96
Serpentine 21, 22, 24, **24,25**
Shaw, Joshua 92
Shifting butt 107
Shot 142

Shot flask 81
Shotgun 1 2, **143**, 154
Shoulder stock 106–107, **106**, **107**
Sights 22
Sling 6, **6**, 66
Smith, Horace 114–115
Snaphaunce **44**, 45–47, **53** 57
Snap-lock 127
Snider, Jacob 132
Spanner, wheel-lock 32–33, **32**
Spear 4
Spear thrower 4
Spring engine **4**, 5
Springfield 63, 150
Steel 45, 46, 48
Stock 17, 22, 50, 51, 53, 54, 62, 64, 66, 77, 78
Afghan **129**
Stockl, Johan **152**
Sub-machine gun 118–119, **119**
Superimposed load 39, 146
Sword 74, **74**
Sword-stick pistol 34

Thompson, General 118
Thynne, Thomas **71**
Tiller 17

Tinder lighter 50
Tommy Gun 118, **119**, 154
Tower of London 14, 15, 78, 90, 108
Tranter, William 102
Trebuchet 4, **4**
Trigger 22, 34, 49, 66, 74, 94, 99, 102
Trigger guard 66, 69, 102, 109
Tripod 19
Tula 60
Tumbler 49, 52

Vienna 60
Von Dreyse, Johan Nikolaus 110

Wad **95**
Walker Colt **99**
Waters, John 73
Webley brothers 104, 105
Wesson, Daniel 114, 115
Wheel-lock **23**, **28**, 29–43, 60, 70, 74, **74**, 76, 84, 108, **116**
accessories 32
workings of 30, **31**
White, Rollin 115
Winchester, Oliver F. 122

SOME OTHER TITLES IN THIS SERIES

Natural History

The Animal Kingdom
Animals of Australia
& New Zealand
Bird Behaviour
Birds of Prey
Evolution of Life
Fishes of the World
Fossil Man

A Guide to the Seashore
Life in the Sea
Mammals of the World
Natural History Collecting
The Plant Kingdom
Prehistoric Animals
Snakes of the World
Wild Cats

Gardening

Chrysanthemums
Garden Flowers

Garden Shrubs
Roses

Popular Science

Astronomy
Atomic Energy
Computers at Work
Electronics

Mathematics
Microscopes & Microscopic Life
The Weather Guide

Arts

Architecture
Jewellery

Porcelain
Victoriana

General Information

Flags
Military Uniforms
Rockets & Missiles
Sailing

Sailing Ships & Sailing Craft
Sea Fishing
Trains
Warships

Domestic Animals and Pets

Budgerigars
Cats
Dog Care

Dogs
Horses & Ponies
Pets for Children

Domestic Science

Flower Arranging

History & Mythology

Discovery of
  Africa
  North America
  The American West
  Japan

Myths & Legends of
  Africa
  Ancient Egypt
  Ancient Greece
  The South Seas